Inter-Generational Youth Ministry:

Why a Balanced View of Connecting the Generations is Essential for the Church

©Copyright 2013 by Mel Walker

Learn more about this book and its author by visiting
www.intergenerationalyouthministry.org and
www.visionforyouth.com

Find other books by Overboard Ministries at
www.overboardministries.com. Comments or
requests for publishing or Overboard Ministry
information should be sent to
overboard@overboardministries.com.

This title is available for your favorite eReader. Visit our
web site, or other online retailers, to choose the format
that is right for you.

Cover design by Alicia Munro
alibo_us@hotmail.com

Interior editing services provided by Lyndsey D Brown.

"Youth workers are by nature 'doers.' But in our passion to 'do' we sometimes forget about our need to engage in the long process of thinking, theorizing, and processing in order to build the strong biblical foundation that must inform our doing. Mel Walker not only challenges us to pause and think deeply before 'doing,' but he asks necessary questions, offers helpful insights that will strengthen our ministries, and gives great practical advice. This is a timely book that deserves our attention."

Walt Mueller, president
Center for Parent/Youth Understanding

"I would love for the sharp younger youth ministry leaders I know to have the opportunity to have a vigorous discussion with Mel Walker. He has extensive youth ministry experience, a passion for Jesus, and sharp mind with contours that are shaped by Biblical truth. So when he dives into the literature and applies himself to improving how local churches practice youth ministry his counsel drips with wisdom. I picture him smiling wide, inviting pushback, and provoking better thought and practice. Fortunately for my youth ministry friends, this book reads like just such a conversation. It's a rich contribution that I pray will help us all become more faithful and effective for the Lord Jesus and kids everywhere."

Dave Rahn, senior VP, chief ministry officer
Youth For Christ

"What a balanced approach to inter-generational youth ministries. It is documented, practical and broad in its scope. It's a great resource for youth workers and church leaders"

Ed Lewis, executive director
CE National

"This is a book that is written for such a time as this. The challenges the church is facing in reaching the next generation is crucial. The model of isolating the generations from one another contradicts clear biblical directives. Mel Walker is a biblical thinker, expert in youth culture, veteran leader in discipleship based youth ministry and an outstanding student of social trends. Most of all, as a friend, co-laborer and fellow church member I can assure you he models what he writes in this insightful work."

Jim Jeffery, president
Baptist Bible College & Seminary

"Mel Walker presents a new approach to solving the problem of kids leaving the church when they graduate high school. After walking through the history of youth ministry, Mel arrives in the present. The value of the book is that he presents real, practical, and Biblical ways to bridge the chasm between the youth ministry and the rest of the church. He shares thoughtful solutions that range from building relationships with adults and parents, to introducing program changes. This will be a valuable resource as we think through how to keep kids involved in church long after their youth ministry years end."

Tim Ahlgrim, national director
Vision For Youth

"This is the direction we need to be going! Mel Walker's *Inter-Generational Youth Ministry* helps us to see the biblical, theological and cultural necessity for connecting generations in our atomized society. But more than that, and here is where Mel has served us well, we are not called to throw out youth and children's ministry, or to lay a heavy burden on ordinary families, but rather we come together - families, youth and children's ministry and the local body of Christ to encourage and welcome young people into the kingdom of God."

Chap Clark, professor & assistant provost
Fuller Theological Seminary

CONTENTS

Dedication

To my wife and best friend, Peggy.

Thanks for living this with me!

Acknowledgements

This project is much more than just a book to me – it's more like a philosophy or a foundational approach to ministry. I have spent a great deal of time doing research (conversations, reading, interviews, visits to churches, and personal observations) in preparation for the finished project. This process has taught me much more than I could ever pass along to readers. This journey towards a true "inter-generational" philosophy of ministry has been lined with a vast host of family members, colleagues, youth workers, pastors, parents, church members, students, and friends.

I know that a brief page of "acknowledgements" can never fully express my thanks for the many, many people who helped me in this process, but it's a good place to start.

My family: To my wife, Peggy; my children Kristi, Todd & Janine, Travis & Kaci; my grandchildren so far (Lana, Ellie, and Haddon) – thank you for your Christ-like love, your loyal support, and your frequent encouragement. I love all of you very much. To my late Dad and Mom, Jim and Louise Walker;– thank you for your Godly legacy of following Christ over the long haul. To my brother, Norm – thank you for your loving example and enduring friendship. My family is undoubtedly the strongest model I know of generation-to-generation of following Christ! I love you all.

My friends and colleagues: I know that I'm in trouble on this one because I don't want to forget anyone, but I want to say a special word of thanks to the team of committed friends who are with me on this journey – Tim Ahlgrim, Don Jackson, and the others involved with Vision For Youth; Jim Jeffery, and my other co-workers at Baptist Bible College & Seminary; Glenn Amos and Jason Jackson, my pastors and friends at Heritage Baptist Church.

To the team at Overboard Ministries: Finally, I want to thank my good friend, Joe Castañeda; my editor Lyndsey Brown; and the staff at Overboard for taking a risk in publishing this book with Vision For Youth!

-Mel

"God is not unjust; He will not forget your work and the love you have shown to Him as you have helped his people and continue to help them." Hebrews 6:10

Introduction

Our kids are leaving the church!

We've all heard the statistics. The number one time people walk away from active involvement in church and their own personal walk with God is following their years in high school.

A wealth of research is out there (and I cite a great deal of it in this book) that provides the proof for this alarming trend, and there are almost as many voices blaming youth ministry for this epidemic. Some blame youth ministry for being entertainment driven, others fault churches for segregating generations, and others criticize youth pastors and youth workers for trying to take the place of Christian parents.

I advocate a balanced view of connecting the generations. In fact, I make the bold claim here that this philosophy is essential for the church! I believe in youth ministry and have spent the majority of life as a youth ministry insider. My children are all actively involved in reaching and ministering to emerging generations; and through my ministries in Christian colleges and Christian organizations, I have invested my life in the training of youth workers and future youth pastors. Obviously, church youth ministry is very, very important to me. I don't believe it is time to eliminate youth ministry in favor of doing something else. There are far too many Biblical and practical reasons not to do that. (Please read the book carefully to hear my rationale for saying that!)

I absolutely and wholeheartedly believe in youth ministry; pastors and other church leaders must make reaching and ministering to the next generation a top priority for the church. Not because the future of the church is in trouble (read Matthew 16:18: *"I will build my church, and the gates of Hades will not overcome it"*); it's not! As Christ tarries, the church will survive, and it will, in fact, thrive. But that's not the point. It's the future of individual kids that is at stake. Youth ministry has long been *a* priority, but is a sound, Biblically-based, and *inter-generational youth ministry* a top priority for the church? I think not. It's time that we make our young people's life-long walk with God our emphasis in the church and in Christian homes.

It's not time to abolish youth ministry. However, it is time to give up on *traditional* youth ministry in favor of a new paradigm and a new model. Tradition is defined as "a long established way of thinking or acting; a continuing pattern of behavior; a customary or characteristic method or manner; the handing down of customs from generation to generation."[1] So, traditional youth ministry (as in this "continuing pattern of behavior") has been characterized by isolating teenagers from the overall life of the church. Certainly, there is some value to this approach. It allows for youth ministry specialists to concentrate on reaching one particular segment of the population and it provides an opportunity for the church to develop culturally relevant methodologies for ministering to future generations. But, perhaps this strategy has inadvertently led to a generation of church dropouts once the kids become young adults.

This book is a call to balance in the church. We must balance the advantages of peer ministry with the importance of connecting the generations. Young people and older people alike need each other. We would fight against segregating our churches over racial or social issues, but we have practiced generational segregation. We must change that tradition in the church. And the way to do that is to develop a balance – build effective youth ministries within a greater context of growing inter-generational relationships and ministry in the church.

I appreciate this observation from *Missional Youth Ministry: Moving from Gathering Teenagers to Scattering Disciples*, by Brian Kirk and Jacob Thome:

> Most teenagers' primary church experience is a series of segregated activities, most of which bear little resemblance to the practices of the rest of the church. Consequently when teenagers graduate from high school and youth group, they feel like their most meaningful church experiences have ended. In short, the program-driven model of youth ministry has failed to help young people find their place in the church.[2]

Let's be intentional about helping the next generation find their place in the church.

Because I think it is important for an author to define his terms for the benefit of the readers, there are three foundational concepts and phrases that I use repeatedly in this book that probably need some definition and explanation. The first is my use of the expression *inter-generational*. I have hyphenated this word on purpose to draw attention to the idea of developing growing and healthy relationships between adults and teenagers in the church. I also use it this way to differentiate inter-generational ministry as a philosophy of ministry from *one-generational* ministry or *multi-generational* ministry models as outlined in Chapter 5.

The second term that deserves clarification is my use of *emerging adults* or *emerging generations*. I borrow this usage from author Jeffrey Jensen Arnett in his work *Emerging Adulthood: The Winding Road from the Late Teens through the Twenties*. Arnett describes emerging adulthood as a prolonged period of life "lasting from the late teens through the mid to late twenties" that is marked by "the rise in the ages of entering marriage and parenthood, the lengthening of higher education, and prolonged job instability." Arnett argues that this extended period of life is new in any type of historical sense, thus it "requires a new term and a new way of thinking."[3]

For a variety of reasons, contemporary culture has extended the period of transition from childhood into adulthood. The Millennial generation and members of "Generation X"[4] before them have been characterized by the seeming lengthening of adolescent issues.

The third term I want to explain is my use of *youth ministry* instead of using the currently popular term *student ministry*. I quote researcher and author Dr. Christian Smith at length because I believe he explains this point much better than I ever could:

> In 2001, when I began to ramp-up my work on the National Study of Youth and Religion (youthandreligion.org) by immersing myself in the world of U.S. ministry to teenagers, I was shocked to learn that the terms youth, youth ministry, and youth minister had been replaced by student, student ministry, and student minister. I don't know how or why the terminology changed – I suspect it has something to do with an undercurrent desire to increase youth ministry's respectability in comparison to other church ministries. In any case, calling teenagers students is a travesty that must stop... Student ministry subtly (and oddly) singles out teenagers from the whole people of God. No church has an 'Employed Adult Ministry' or a 'Home-maker Minister' or 'Retired Seniors Minister.' So why should the church define its

ministry to youth around the institutional social status of student? I think this label subtly isolates youth as a subculture to be treated differently. The church needs to be moving in the exact opposite direction when it comes to teenagers... I'm asking Christian youth workers all over the country to change your shaping language—to use language that honors teenagers as whole human persons in God's kingdom. Please stop calling teenagers students, and ask everyone around you to do the same.[5]

Though I understand why the term *student ministry* has been popular in recent years, like Smith, I believe that *youth ministry* more accurately reflects the purpose of this ministry.

Our kids may be leaving the church following their graduation from high school, but we must not accept this trend as the status quo or we will become bound by our cultural traditions instead of believing that our all-loving, omnipotent, sovereign God can change things for His glory and for the eternal good of generation after generation of Christ-followers. The basic reason why I love youth ministry so much is that it gives us an enduring hope for the future – that God can use emerging generations to change things in the church and that our God will continue to bless and use His church, the *Body of Christ* and the *Bride of Christ*, to impact future generations!

Chapter One: Generation Gap
Why Can't We All Just Get Along?

Walk with me on a Sunday morning tour around most traditional churches in this country. The children are gathered with their dutiful Sunday school teachers in various classrooms around the basement. A group of teenagers meets with a couple of youthful-looking adult leaders in the living room of an old house next door, while most of the adults are scattered throughout the auditorium. A cluster of senior citizens gathers in the pastor's office in arranged rows of folding metal chairs. Other than the involvement of a few loyal church workers, the various generations have almost nothing to do with each other during the church's Sunday school hour.

Sadly, the morning service demonstrates the same basic approach. Some young parents reserve seats for their children, but many of the teenagers gather with other teenagers. Most of the older adults sit with other older adults, and a few families sit together in almost assigned-seating patterns of familiarity. You can imagine what happens next. The song leader has the people turn in the hymnals to sing a few of the time-honored hymns. The pastor leads in prayer and then gives a few announcements before the offering and before the children leave to return to the basement for their church-time programming. The song leader then returns, this time using a portable data projector to display the words of a handful of choruses and the pastor heads to the pulpit to preach the morning sermon.

On this fictional tour with me, I'm wondering if you noticed anything familiar along the way. Many of us have grown up in the era of age-segregated church ministry, and it's happening now in smaller churches and mega-churches alike.

Somewhere along the line we have accepted the idea that it is a good thing to separate the various generations, to the exclusion of developing healthy inter-generational relationships in the church.

Please don't get me wrong. I am a long-time advocate of local church youth ministry. I believe in it and can argue its merits both Biblically and practically. (We'll discuss the advantages and virtues of peer-to-peer, age-group based ministry as we move throughout this book.) However, I have come to the conclusion that if the generations are totally disconnected from each other in the church, we are making a tragic and long-lasting mistake. The basic premise of this book is a call to balance. We dare not overreact. Doing away with peer ministry (e.g., children's ministry and youth ministry) also yields disastrous results. (We'll also take a look at the current trend to do away with age-based ministries later on in the book.)

As researchers Brenda Snailum and Brad Griffin report, "Establishing inter-generational community does not mean eradicating age-specific ministries. As important as it is to embrace inter-generational values at a core level, it's also important to keep that in balance with age-specific ministry." Griffin and Snailum add that although ministry to specific age groups may be "working" to some extent, "all ages still need their own space to grow and develop at their own pace. Everyone needs to be part of a web of relationships that includes their peers AND members of other generations."[6]

Where did we get the idea that it is a good thing to separate the generations? I believe that the current traditional church structure, where we almost totally disconnect the generations from each other, actually is a fairly recent trend that has been adapted from cultural and even secular customs. Here are some possible causes of an age-segregated "generation gap" in the church:

Religious Influences

The Universal Acceptance of Sunday School

One of the most obvious originators of age-segregated ministry was the wide acceptance of the Sunday school as an essential ingredient of church educational endeavors. Beginning in Britain in the 1780s, the Sunday school movement was heavily influenced by the Industrial Revolution, which resulted in many children working all week in factories, including Saturdays. As Timothy Larson notes, "Sunday, therefore, was the only available time for these children to gain some education." The movement quickly spread to America and soon "denominations and non-denominational organizations caught the vision and energetically began to create Sunday schools. Within decades, the movement had become extremely popular." Larson adds that by the mid-19th century, "Sunday school attendance was a near universal aspect of childhood. Even parents who did not regularly attend church themselves generally insisted that their children go to Sunday school."[7]

Though general education was the original goal of the Sunday school movement, by the early 1800s, Sunday schools began focusing on the "regeneration and conversion of children," with an emphasis on teaching the gospel and doctrine. In the United States, "the first national Sunday school effort began in 1824; its stated purpose was to organize, evangelize and civilize. The focus was intentionally evangelical, and so within the next 100 years the Sunday school had become the primary outreach arm of the church. The Sunday school organization (soon) expanded to include all ages."[8]

Along with the rise in popularity of the Sunday school came the corresponding professionalism and administration of institutionalism. Soon evangelical publishers saw the need and opportunity to create and publish age-specific educational materials to assist this growing phenomenon. Traditional churches almost universally accepted the idea that it was a positive pro-

3

gramming strategy to separate the various age groups around specific age-related educational abilities and needs. Different instructional methods were used for children, youth, and adults – often various stages of these age categories were also separated even further into sub groups for the goal of more effective learning. In fact, I spent almost 10 years of my life leading in the development of junior high and senior high Sunday school and youth group meeting materials and curriculum.

The Subtle Influence of Jewish Tradition

Ancient Jewish tradition (along with other Eastern and Mid-Eastern societies) included a specific *rite of passage* from childhood into cultural adulthood. A Wikipedia entry puts it this way, "Rites of passage are often ceremonies surrounding events such as other milestones within puberty, coming of age, marriage and death. Initiation ceremonies such as baptism, confirmation and *Bar* or *Bat Mitzvah* are considered important rites of passage for people of their respective religions."[9] This "coming of age" custom is vividly illustrated in Scripture when Jesus' human parents took him to the Temple in Jerusalem as a 12-year old. (The narrative is found in Luke 2:41-52, while this Jewish regulation is explained in Deuteronomy 16:16.) The early chapters in Luke's Gospel present Christ as a child, while the later chapters tell the accounts of Him as an adult. The historical disconnect between generations was well defined by this coming of age cultural benchmark.

The contemporary church has, perhaps unwittingly, accepted and adopted this ancient practice of separating children from adults – especially educationally. It seems we have bought into the idea that spiritual formation and development happens best in an age-specific environment. There are, as mentioned above, some advantages of peer-with-peer learning. Students can interact and learn alongside people their own age, often with similar educational and life experiences (e.g., first graders learning along with other first graders and teenagers meeting with other teenagers). However, the drawbacks of dividing the church generationally are especially obvious and egregious when we take into consideration that our graduating high school seniors have never developed healthy, growing relationships with very many people outside their own age group. It's no wonder kids grow up and walk away from the church.

Cultural Influences

The term "generation gap" became popular in the United States during the 1950s and 1960s, referring to the generational differences between children and their parents.[10] However, the basic differences between generations can be traced further back than that. Obviously, each generation shares mutually-experienced life events and influences and that has been the case throughout history. In fact, Franklin Delano Roosevelt commented in 1936 that "there is a mysterious cycle in human events. To some generations much is given. Of other generations much is expected."[11] (Perhaps the most definitive research on the subject of generational characteristics has been done by Neil Howe and William Strauss. See the bibliography for a general listing of some of their work.[12]) Recent western culture has been dramatically defined by sweeping generational divisions that have influenced traditional church programming as well.

The Industrial Revolution

As mentioned above, the Industrial Revolution was a cultural game-changer for both society in general and for the church in particular. In its early stages, children, especially adolescents, were viewed as extra workers in the escalating industrialized workforce. One writer puts it this way, "The factory system changed the manner in which work was performed. Unlike the domestic system the work was away from home, in large, impersonal settings. Workers were viewed by their employers merely as 'hands.'"[13] The church, in typical fashion, ultimately responded to this significant cultural shift with a change in its basic programming and structure. The institution of an age-divided Sunday school was one such reaction.

Compulsory Education

In the United States, compulsory education first began in Massachusetts in 1852 and became a law in every state by 1918. Although the original law mandated that children attend public school, many states now allow children to fulfill their education requirements in private or home school settings.[14] Early proponents of this philosophy included educators such as Horace Mann[15] and Thomas Dewey,[16] who both championed the idea of mandatory government-sponsored public schooling.

While compulsory education was obviously useful, in that it provided children an opportunity and environment in which to learn, the system also fostered the idea of age-based segregation. Earlier educational methodologies were centered around a strong parental influence over children. Parents, often fathers, were actively involved in their children's education and vocational training (see Ephesians 6:4). This hands-on connection with close adults provided tangible inter-generational relationships. Once children were separated from their parents for several hours each day, their closest interpersonal relationships became with their peers – who vastly outnumbered their teachers.

Soon the church accepted and implemented that age-specific educational approach. Sunday schools, youth groups, and children's clubs became a common practice that divided the generations for age-specific programming. Adult educational ministries followed, and the traditional church rapidly became disconnected generationally.

Child Labor Laws

Child labor laws in the early twentieth century also created an unintended generational detachment. As the number of child laborers spiked near the turn of the century, various reform groups began pushing for stricter labor standards and improved conditions, thus giving more power and rights to the workers. This movement eventually resulted in the National Child Labor Committee in 1904, which opposed child labor and implemented anti-sweatshop campaigns. Eventually, the Fair Labor Standards Act of 1938 set nation-wide standards for child labor, such as a maximum workweek and an established minimum wage.[17]

Though the Fair Labor Standards Act rightfully protected children from oppressive work conditions, it also separated them from other age groups. Where the younger generations once worked alongside of their parents and other adults, the Child Labor Laws actually helped create a set of new experiences for young people. They now had extra time on their hands to spend with their peers. This newly established youth culture, although developed with the best intentions in mind (protecting kids from difficult working conditions), actually may have led to a somewhat negative outcome. Youth suddenly had more and more relational connections with each other and less and less time to develop close relationships with adults.

The church reacted to this trend as well. Since teenagers had so much free time, the church saw the need to help fill that gap. It made sense for churches to organize events and activities for youth since they had nothing else to do. Soon communities and churches all around the country were planning and hosting after-school and weekend programs for young people.

Juvenile Justice System

The other cultural trend that may have created the gap between generations was the development of this country's juvenile justice system. Prior to the Progressive Era, a period of social activism in the late nineteenth and early twentieth century, child over the age of seven convicted of crimes were imprisoned with adults. However, as a result of political and social reforms, in addition to growing research from psychologists in the eighteenth and nineteenth century, society became increasingly interested in reforming children instead of just punishing them. One website describes the system this way:

> Such early changes to the justice system were made under a newfound conviction that society had a responsibility to recover the lives of its young offenders before they became absorbed in the criminal activity they were taking part in. The juvenile justice system exercised its authority within a "*parens patriae*" (state as parent or guardian) role. The state assumed the responsibility of parenting the children until they began to exhibit positive changes, or became adults. Youth were no longer tried as adult offenders. Their cases were heard in a somewhat informal court designed for juveniles, often without the assistance of attorneys. Extenuating evidence, outside of the legal facts surrounding the crime or delinquent behavior, was taken into consideration by the judge. Early reform houses were, in many ways, similar to orphanages. Indeed, many of the youth housed in the reformatories were orphans and homeless children.[18]

This shift in thinking, from believing children should be tried similarly to adults to advocating for alternative "age-appropriate" punishments, perhaps also led to a growing segregation of generations. Certainly it made sense to protect juveniles from incarceration with hardened adult criminals, and it seemed logical to steer children and youth away from anti-social behavior. However, the same research that led society to adapt the juvenile justice system also led to the general sentiment that youth are intrinsically and fundamentally different than adults and should be treated differently by all institutions – including the church.

It is no wonder then that the children gather in the basement and the teenagers meet separately from adults. Culture has convinced us that it's a good idea. However, as we move through the 21st century, maybe the cultural trends should change. As we will discuss later on, the Bible does not present an age-specific church. The fact is, the generations need each other. And since so many of our churched youth are leaving the church following high school graduation, maybe the church will react to this unsettling trend by making some significant changes in its programs and structure.

Kara Powell, a youth ministry professor and researcher, observes that the "one thing churches can do that really makes a difference is getting kids actively involved in the life of the church before they graduate. There is a strong link between kids staying in church after they graduate and their involvement in inter-generational relationships."[19]

Perhaps it's time to change things in your church!

Chapter Two: The Invention of the Teenager
How Traditional Youth Ministry Got It Wrong

The year was 1944. In many ways, it was the beginning of the end. In other ways, this one particular year was truly just the beginning of what was to become a cultural phenomenon that impacted both secular and religious culture for decades to come – the development of a nationwide youth culture. On June 6, 1944, the Allied troops launched the largest invasion force in history onto the beaches of Normandy, France, in what became known as "D-Day" – literally the beginning of the end of World War II. Certainly, the events surrounding that massive assault dominate the history books chronicling the year 1944. But, if we track other significant influences that also occurred that year we would have to include the construction of the world's first digital computer at Harvard University, the first scientific identification of DNA, and Congress' passing of what was to become the "GI Bill," to help returning soldiers assimilate back into American society.[20]

However, there was another interesting cultural development in September 1944, and that was the publication of the first issue of *Seventeen* magazine. Here's what author Jon Savage, in *Teenage: The Creation of Youth Culture,* reports about the beginning of this new publication: "In September 1944, a magazine was launched that pulled together the strands of democracy, national identity, peer culture, target marketing, and youth consumerism into an irresistible package."[21] It is interesting that Savage also identifies this one event as a catalyst for an entirely new way of thinking. Savage goes onto explain that "the increasing importance of youth demanded a new name. That America had a unique way of organizing its adolescents had already been recognized by the sociologist Talcott Parsons. In an October 1942 article...he coined the term 'youth culture' to describe the particular 'set of patterns and behavior phenomena' that was unique to American society." Savage continues, "During 1944, the words 'teenage' and 'teenager' became the accepted way to describe this new definition of youth as a discrete, mass market. Teenagers were neither adolescents nor juvenile delinquents. Consumerism offered the perfect counterbalance to riot and rebellion: it was the American way of harmlessly diverting youth's disruptive energies."[22]

This era may have been the perfect storm of convergence of cultural factors that led to the emergence of a new youth culture in America. The war was soon to end and its conclusion meant a tidal wave of young people moving back into a society that was already featuring a growing generation gap of workers. Gary McIntosh writes about the generational influences in the post-war society: "The early boom of babies following World War II was at first not surprising. A rise in the birth rate after the 'boys came home' was expected. Within a few years however, the staggering growth of four million babies a year alerted observers that something different was taking place. One thing was certain – the babies kept coming and coming and coming."[22]

The war and post-war years also triggered a new kind of youth culture. Dean Borgman of Gordon-Conwell Theological Seminary notes that "what the Depression had begun, World War II accelerated...Teenagers were 'the biggest men in town.' And they had money in a new booming economy. With this new label of *teenager* and money to spend, they quickly caught the merchants' eyes, and teen magazines, music, and clothes were soon on the market."[23]

Parachurch Organizations

God's people responded to this growing cultural influence *en masse*. Probably the initial youth ministry strategy was the development of the youth rally as a means to reach and minister to teenagers. One youth ministry expert described what was happening this way:

> As the war wound down, the response…increased. Thirty thousand crowded into Chicago Stadium for a 'Victory Rally' in the fall of 1944. Twenty thousand packed Madison Square Garden for one of Jack Wyrtzen's 'Word of Life' rallies as another 10,000 people were turned away… The movement spread so effectively and rapidly that one might look for a master strategy formulated by a few people and implemented by others in their organizations. But such was not true. The youth rally idea was a grassroots movement which spread like a grass fire.[24]

Another early response that same year to America's looming youth culture was the development of youth centers which dotted the country's landscape. Savage observes that "the way forward was shown by a May 1944 feature in *Look*, which described the successful campaign run by Ruth Clifton, editor of the high school paper in Moline, Illinois, to open a youth center. Concerned about the number of adolescents…she successfully petitioned the city council to renovate an empty warehouse." Savage explains, "Picturing the new center full of adolescents drinking Cokes, the copy noted, 'how juvenile delinquency can be decreased by mobilization of the energies and creativeness of youth people. Young America knows it own difficulties; it will solve them, given a chance.'"[25]

God's people also responded to this movement to create youth centers. Here's one example from youth ministry historian Mark Senter: "Lloyd T. Bryant of New York City appears to have been the originator of a youth-targeted mass evangelization effort in the United States. (As the first full-time minister to youth at Manhattan's Calvary Baptist Church) his motto was 'training through participation' and student involvement in evangelistic efforts was the key...Youth centers were at the heart of Bryant's approach to youth ministry."[26]

Another historical event that happened in 1944 which merits our consideration in this discussion on the development of a youth culture in this country, including the church's response, is the beginning of a world-wide youth ministry organization that year aptly named Youth For Christ. The organization began at the Winona Lake Bible Conference in Winona Lake, Indiana, when a group wanted to create new ministry events for youth. Youth For Christ eventually emerged from the planning and Chicago pastor Torrey Johnson was elected chairman.[27]

An interesting source of more information on the history of youth ministry (and many other aspects of evangelical Christianity) can be found in the archives of the Billy Graham Evangelistic Center at Wheaton College (see http://www.wheaton.edu/bgc/archives). Here is one post on the early history of Youth For Christ:

> During World War II, pastors in widely separated cities in the United States and Canada began holding huge evangelistic rallies especially aimed at young people, including those in the armed forces. These rallies had been inspired by the youth work of men like Paul Guiness and Jack Wyrtzen, and included entertainment, singing, and vigorous preaching. Among the more important leaders of the movement were...Jack Wyrtzen from New York...and Torrey Johnson from Chicago. In August of 1944...these men and others...met at Winona Lake, Indiana, to form a temporary organization to serve as a channel for the various rallies to render mutual assistance to each other...Torrey Johnson was elected the chairman of a temporary committee. Johnson soon recruited Billy

Graham, who had worked on the Chicago rallies, to become the organizations' first full-time evangelist. A magazine also began to be published...Less than a year later, 42 delegates from the various rallies met again at Winona Lake to make Youth for Christ International (YFCI) into a permanent organization.[28]

Though Dean Borgman notes that skeptics considered the organization "a passing fad, and critics found its excesses and mistakes...Youth For Christ became and continues to be a mighty force for youth evangelism around the world."[29]

Other youth ministry organizations and initiatives soon followed. All of them were incredibly creative, culturally relevant, and were designed to reach out to teenagers within this emerging youth culture. The early developers of youth ministries tended to be visionary entrepreneurs with a compelling desire to see young people come to Christ. They saw a developing cultural trend and were highly motivated to do something about it. Their zeal and enthusiasm soon out-distanced established church leaders who tended to be more conservative and more concerned with ministering to adults than they were about evangelizing teenagers. Therefore, this group of influential leaders often took the opportunity to create their own parachurch organizations instead of working inside the traditional church structure. Over the course of the next decade or two, some of the most significant and long-lasting youth ministry organizations got their start. These parachurch organizations included Lloyd Bryant's youth centers, Youth for Christ, Word of Life, Young Life, and Awana.[30]

Over the next few years, two other noteworthy youth ministry trends were also established. The first was the rise of the professional youth worker. Senter wrote that "thousands of people influenced by the movement either went directly into the ministry or enrolled at Bible institutes and colleges, Christian liberal arts schools, and seminaries." Senter continues, noting that by the early 1950's, "thousands of people were committed to doing professional youth ministry. The vast majority of these people found places of service in the emerging parachurch youth ministry agencies...The number of people employed to do Christian youth ministry suggests that the youth movement had become a profession."[31]

Soon Christian colleges followed suit and instituted specialized academic programs for people headed into vocational youth ministry. Liberty University (then Lynchburg Baptist College) is often credited as being the first Christian college in the United States to offer a youth ministry major in 1971.[32] Here's what Gordon Luff, Liberty's first youth ministry professor, recalls: "[The Liberty] philosophy is very distinct. It's a movement that said traditional methods of church youth work were not working and new and innovative ideas were necessary to change that. The primary one being the training of a professional person to lead the youth program, and that necessitates at least a college degree."[33]

The other notable trend was the production of printed materials for the growing youth ministry market. Within a few years, major Christian publishers began to publish curricula and resources for this mounting new emphasis. Companies such as Scripture Press and David C. Cook launched distinct new lines of youth ministry products.[34] Soon entire new organizations were created to cater to the newly established youth ministry industry. The early leaders of these specialized organizations were Youth Specialties and Group Publishing. Both companies were formed to provide products and services that met the needs of this new ministry discipline.[35]

I grew up in the days of monthly youth rallies sponsored by Youth for Christ and the annual two-week evangelistic campaigns with Word of Life founder Jack Wyrtzen. Although this approach seemed to fit the culture better then, today's students are searching for more than a periodic sermon or a series of meetings. They need real answers to tough questions and they long to be confident of what they believe and how to back up those beliefs from Scripture. Even though modern youth ministry has downplayed the methodology of the occasional youth rally, I'm not sure it has been replaced with anything more substantial. The trend in churches today seems to be a lack of emphasis upon traditional Christian educational ministries or preaching in lieu of interaction, entertainment, or performance-based programming. In Christian Smith's oft-quoted treatise *Soul Searching: The Religious and Spiritual Lives of American Teenagers*, he writes, "The vast majority of US teenagers embrace some religious identity...[but do not have] particularly well-articulated beliefs about their own religious traditions."[36] I think that's why this is a generation that is looking to go *deeper*, spiritually-speaking. They can be entertained elsewhere. They are craving answers and depth from the Scriptures and they expect the church to deliver.

The Church

As we discussed in Chapter 1, the church seems to copy and imitate the cultural and organizational trends of other influences. Society created a youth culture and the church responded to it. Here, we've seen that parachurch ministries led the way in the development of relevant means to reach out to the emerging trend of youth ministry – and again the church reacted to it.

These ministries identified a need in society (the growing youth culture) and developed culturally-relevant ways to reach out to teenagers. Youth centers, youth rallies, youth clubs, and youth materials were instituted. Parachurch organizations were also hiring youth ministry professionals and the church ultimately did the same.

Senter observes, "Much like the sudden appearance of the rock 'n roll disc jockey, the youth pastor was a response to the vocal presence of middle class adolescents as factors in the American way of life." Senter goes onto argue that "so compelling was the teenage generation that, had Young Life and Youth for Christ not been present, youth pastors would have appeared on the scene anyway, but their ministry values and philosophy would have come from a different source. The parachurch agencies were there, however, and as a result played a formative role in the development of the profession."[37]

Youth ministry had become *en vogue*, and a new church emphasis was born. Churches saw the need for youth ministry as a conduit for growth and relevancy, and thousands of churches all around the country began to hire trained vocational youth pastors. If churches didn't have the size or resources to hire a professional youth pastor, they still modeled their youth programs as if they did, and instead recruited lay volunteers to serve in the capacity of youth leaders or youth sponsors. Churches wanted to reach their communities for Christ and wanted to minister to the parents and families of teenagers, and therefore made youth ministry a priority for facility use, budgeting, and people resources (often the church's best workers were steered toward working with teenagers). Yes, youth ministry was here to stay. It became a tradition in the church, and more and more, churches separated the teenagers from the other generations.

Did We Get It Wrong?

Each of the trends identified in this chapter may have inadvertently helped to form a generationally-segregated church. Making youth ministry a specialization certainly seemed like the right thing to do. Professional youth pastors and other youth experts could reach a newly-defined youth culture by concentrating on this one particular age group. Many of these vocational youth workers sensed a God-given call to youth ministry and many dedicated their lives in specializing on one age group – teenagers.

It made sense to hire specialists, experts, if you will, who were trained, experienced, and dedicated to working with youth. The new generation of young people and society's interest in marketing to this emerging demographic cohort created an influential and powerful youth culture. Teenagers began to be featured in movies, magazines, and in the news. The pop music and fashion industries followed. The youth culture was big business. Churches recognized that they needed experts to handle the growing needs of a new generation. They responded by hiring youth pastors and making youth ministry a top priority.

But, something negative happened along the way. No longer could just anyone work with teenagers. Youth workers needed to be trained professionals. They needed to be specialists. They should be equipped and *called* to work with this needy age group. Teenagers were a different breed. They were no longer children but not yet adults. They needed separate meeting spaces, and they had their own musical tastes and their own fashion fads. Teenagers were different than other generations. It made sense to segregate them from the other age groups. And so, the era of age-specific ministries became entrenched in the church. It became tradition to separate the generations. It became our practice, our custom.

I have been amazed during my travels around the country at just how segregated many churches have become. Often the youth meeting space is as far away as possible from where the adults meet. I visited a large denominational church in the Midwest a few years ago that was building a large youth ministry building on their campus. This facility was indeed impressive. It had a full-size gym, several large classrooms, a concert stage, and numerous offices. It even had its own Starbucks. However, I couldn't help but notice that the structure was as far away as possible from the main auditorium. Even a casual observer would notice that they wanted the youth to be separated from the other generations.

As a veteran of local church youth ministry, I have spent over 35 years of my professional life specializing in student ministry. I appreciate peer ministry and can expound its virtues. We'll see in the next chapter how the Bible emphasizes reaching the next generation and passing along truth and faith from generation-to-generation. But, totally separating the generations may have been an overreaction. Yes, there are huge advantages for age group specialization, but there are disadvantages, too. Perhaps the church overreacted by convincing herself that teenagers did not need much inter-generational interaction.

Maybe we got it wrong. Youth ministry came of age "because of the passion that women and men had for passing on the faith from one generation to another."[38] But, is there a better way? Let's start with the Bible.

Chapter Three: Passing the Baton
The Generation-to-Generation Principle in Scripture

From the memorial of stones in the Jordan River to the Apostle Paul's final instruction to his student Timothy, and from the Garden of Eden to the churches listed in The Revelation, the Biblical model is generation-to-generation ministry. God Himself intended truth and faith to be passed down the line of time as long as Christ tarries, from one generation to the next. That was His plan for humanity. Each generation is to reproduce itself spiritually in the lives of the next generation. One generation must "talk it and walk it" and the next generation has to "catch it and match it."

You know the story. The Nation of Israel was finally about to enter the Promised Land. One barrier remained – the Jordan River. (You can read and study the narrative on your own in Joshua 3 and 4.) God miraculously parted the water and the hundreds of thousands of Israelites were able to cross the river on dry ground. God had kept His promise. He delivered them out of Egypt, across the Red Sea, through the wilderness, and now into the Promised Land. It was then that God instructed Joshua to build a monument or a memorial there in the Jordan River that would be a tangible, visible reminder of God's blessing and provision for generations to come. It's here in the sequence that the Bible gives this classic illustration on the importance of making sure that each generation *gets it* – that each successive generation understands and remembers what God did for His people. You can read the account in Joshua 4:21-24. Here's the point: In the days ahead when children would notice the monument, they'd ask their parents, "What do these stones mean?" Then the parents would have the privilege to tell them what God did in bringing the nation out of bondage and into the new land. This visual aid gave the parents the opportunity to share the story from generation to generation – *"That all the peoples of the earth may know that the hand of the LORD is mighty, so that you may fear the LORD your God forever."*

The generation-to-generation principle is interwoven throughout the pages of Scripture and includes an indication of the heartbeat of the Apostle Paul when we realize that his last recorded letter in the Bible was written to a young man, a student if you will, Timothy. The Epistle of 2 Timothy was written not to a peer, not to a fellow Apostle, and not to a church or group of churches. Instead, it was written to a young man – a man Paul had invested his life in throughout many of his journeys. Scholars tell us that Paul wrote this letter from a dungeon prison in Rome where he was about to be martyred for his faith in Christ. It's interesting to me that one of Paul's major concerns in this letter is that the work of the ministry would go on and prosper. You'll remember the familiar challenge in 2 Timothy 2:2, *"And the things you have heard me say in the presence of many witnesses entrust to reliable men who will also be qualified to teach others."*

In this final pep talk to his student, Paul wanted Timothy to keep this process of ministry going. Notice the four generations indicated in this one verse – the first generation was Paul, the second was Timothy, the third was referred to as "reliable men," and the fourth generation was the "others." Paul had discipled Timothy (see 2 Timothy 3:10-17) and now he was instructing Timothy to disciple others.

This too illustrates the soundness and the practicality of this principle – the work carries on. From Old Testament patriarchs building memorials for future generations, to New Testament Apostles instructing students to continue making disciples – the Bible is permeated with practical illustrations and workable instructions on how each generation is to reproduce itself in the lives of the next generation.

For our purposes in this book, let's take a look at the two basic institutions the Scriptures have established as conduits of that process: the family and the church. Parents are to pass the baton to their children, and the church likewise is to make the transference from one generation to the next.

The Family

God established the family unit in His creation of the universe. Mankind was told to *"be fruitful and multiply"* in Genesis 1:28, and the process by which that would be accomplished is further explained in Genesis 2:20-25 with the creation of man and woman. Of course, students of the Genesis narrative will recall how sin entered the world shortly thereafter, but even the reproduction of the sin nature (see Romans 5:12) is somewhat of an illustration of this generation-to-generation progression. Very soon the family became the most obvious building block of the emerging civilization. Most of the Old Testament is a collection of the stories of families, such as the running narrative of what became God's chosen people – the Nation of Israel. The pages of the Old Testament reveal that life itself and faith in the Creator God of the Universe had to be passed down the line from one generation to another.

Reggie Joiner, the founder of the *Think Orange* movement, summarizes the foundational importance of family in the Bible this way:

> I used to wonder why so much genealogy was included in the Old Testament; those Scripture passages don't contain a lot of profound revelations or much that seems relevant to my daily issues. However, I realize now that these lists display family after family and generation after generation to show that every family and every generation was connected to God's story. You can see the continuation of God's redemptive plan as it unfolds in the Hebrew family

tree from Adam to Jesus, from Genesis to Matthew...God's promises and commandments were
passed from one generation to the next through the
conduit of the family.[39]

Generation-to-generation connections were especially
true within the Jewish culture. Passages such as Deuteronomy
4:9, *"Only be careful, and watch yourselves closely so that you do not
forget the things your eyes have seen or let them slip from your heart
as long as you live. Teach them to your children and to their children
after them,"* give credence to this plan for parents (in the Jewish
tradition, especially fathers) to teach obedience to the commands of God to each succeeding generation.

This plan is amplified in the familiar *Shema* passage in
Deuteronomy 6. A simple reading of this account shows the parental responsibility to teach their children to *"Love the LORD
your God with all your heart and with all your soul and with all your
strength."* Notice that this was to be an intentional strategy. Everyday life was to be centered upon training and educational activities and initiatives. The end of this chapter reiterates the passage of truth and tradition from one generation to another.
Verses 20-25 point out that there will come times when future
generations will need to hear the great historical stories of all
that God did. This same theme is repeated in passages such as
Psalm 78:1-8. One generation is to help the next generation "not
forget" the works of God.

There is something very powerful when parents share
God stories with their children. We have the Biblical responsibility to remind our children of the great things God has done and
is doing throughout history. This too should be an intentional
and strategic venture for all Christian parents. This process is in
actuality making sure that the Lord is the top priority in our
lives and in our homes. Let's never forget that the primary focus
of the *Shema* in Deuteronomy 6:5 is for us as parents to love God

and make Him the center of our lives. Only then can we adequately and completely teach that focus to our children.

Parents, this begins with us. If we want our kids to go on for God as they progress throughout childhood and into their adult lives, it is imperative that we show them that living consistently for the Lord is what our lives are all about. As my daughter often reminds me, there's only one thing you can say before saying "Lord," and that is "Yes!" Our lives and our instruction to our children must be a living and consistent reflection that Christ is indeed the *Lord* of our lives – only then will we be able to translate that faith to the next generation.

The Church

Well-known Biblical scholar Dr. Charles Ryrie argues that "the home and the church are the only two God-ordained 'institutions' for carrying out His work. This is not to say that God does not use other organizations in His program, but it is to emphasize that the church is of primary importance in His purpose. When we abandon the church we abandon God's organization."[40] Robert Saucy puts it his way, "[The church] is the primary instrument through which He ministers in the world."[41]

Christian parents certainly have the almost daunting responsibility to raise our kids in the *"nurture and admonition of the Lord"* (KJV). (See Ephesians 6:4.) Biblically, the responsibility for the spiritual growth and maturity falls squarely upon the parents. However, the God-given purpose of His church is to develop, as Bill Hybels puts it, "fully devoted followers of Christ."[42] I quote Hybels's perhaps over-used mission statement here, not as an endorsement of the Willow Creek seeker-sensitive philosophy, but to help readers readily recall the grand mission of the church. The church exists to help God's people in their journey to spiritual maturity (see Ephesians 4:11-16, 2 Timothy 3:10-17, Matthew 28:18-20).

In other words, people need the church; as one author puts it, "it takes a church to raise a Christian."[43] Or, as Ryrie succinctly states, "The purpose of the church is to produce mature, stable, holy Christians."[44]

It's also important to note that the church is God's agency for carrying out His Great Commission (Matthew 28:19-20, Mark 16:15, and Acts 1:8). This is His global plan for all people, for all time. And, the church is His only plan. We must never come to the conclusion that the church is archaic and irrelevant, or that it is boring and ineffective. The church is the *bride of Christ* (Ephesians 5:25-33 and Revelation 19:7-8) and is His *body* (1 Corinthians 12). It doesn't make sense that Christ followers would be critical or negative about something so near and dear to the heart of God, even if some say *They Like Jesus, But Not the Church.*[45] We really don't have that option.

Here's the point. Our kids need the church to grow spiritually as Christ intended. Parents must raise their children in the "training and instruction of the Lord" (Ephesians 6:4), but God wants His church to be a part of that process.

I love the story in Scripture of John Mark. He was a young man who grew up in a Christian home, but he also grew up in church (see Acts 12:12). It's interesting to note that, as a student, he was selected to go along on the first missionary trip ever (Acts 13:5). John Mark was a young man with an incredible future. The early church met in his parents' home and his formative years included the influence of Godly Christian leaders like Pater, Paul, and Barnabas. Yet, he went through some bumps along the way. There was the infamous situation in Perga (see Acts 13:13) when he quit the missionary team and went back home. This quitter then caused the divisive argument between the Apostle Paul and missionary team leader, Barnabas (Acts 15:36-41).

I can identify with John Mark because, like him, I too was a church kid who grew up in a Christian home. I went through some bumps along the way, too. There were times I'm sure, when my parents and other influential people in my life thought I'd never amount to anything spiritually. But, God had a different plan for my life and He did for John Mark's life also. Ultimately, God used him to be the human writer of one of the books of Scripture (the Gospel of Mark) and even the Apostle Paul, the one who didn't want to take this quitter on the next missions trip, refers to John Mark as someone "helpful to me in my ministry" (2 Timothy 4:11).

Readers, isn't that want we want from the next generation? We want them to go on for God as adults. Let's go back to the Old Testament for a vivid illustration of the antithesis of the story of John Mark. In Judges 2, God's Word presents the sad account of a generation that did not go on for God: *"Another generation grew up, who knew neither the Lord nor what he had done for Israel"* (v. 10). In my opinion, this is one of the saddest stories in the Bible. One generation failed to spiritually reproduce themselves in the lives of the next generation and the nation of Israel, in God's sovereignty of course, suffered through the many years of failures and victories as chronicled for us in the book of Judges.

It is powerful and incredibly positive when the home and the church work together to help the next generation go on for Him. We'll take a look at how that works in the next chapter.

Chapter Four: It Takes a Church
When Parents and the Church Actually Work Together

Several years ago Hillary Clinton caused quite a stir, especially among her vast right-wing antagonists, for her bestselling book, *It Takes a Village & Other Lessons Children Teach Us*. She chose an ancient African proverb as inspiration for her work. Although conservative talk-show hosts and an almost infinite number of other critics blasted her for failing to put the ultimate responsibility of raising children squarely upon the shoulders of parents, perhaps she did have a very good point. Ted Bolsinger, the pastor of San Clemente Presbyterian Church in San Clemente, California, agrees: "In a similar way that the proverb reveals the necessity of a community to raise healthy children in an often hostile world, the process of spiritual growth and transformation is an even more intensely communal activity."[46]

I think most readers of this book would agree that Christ followers need the church. We have had the truth of Hebrews 10:25, *"Not forsaking the assembling of ourselves together, as the manner of some is... (KJV)*, drilled into our minds, via ever-present Scripture memory programs. We understand the importance of body-life functions in the church such as meeting together, corporate worship, and the preaching and teaching of the Word of God. However, I'm not sure that we're convinced of the *relevance* of the church in today's culture.

According to creationist lecturer Ken Ham, the majority of today's young adults do not believe the church is relevant.[47] Ham also quotes pollster George Barna who revealed that "nearly 70%" of "twentysomethings" were "significantly less likely to believe that a person's faith in God is meant to be developed by involvement in a local church."[48] Popular speaker and author Dan Kimball reaffirms this notion and adds weight to this negative trend: "Two-thirds of those who graduate from high school...end up leaving their church."[49]

The Power of Collaboration

I understand that many, many other voices have shared their ideas about how to reverse this movement among emerging generations away from regular involvement in church. I too will share other specific thoughts on this subject later on in the book. However, I am absolutely convinced that the collaborative influence of the family and the church working together can and will have a powerful and prevailing impact upon the next generation. (For more information on the general subject of *collaboration* from a secular viewpoint, take a look at *Swarm Creativity: Competitive Advantage through Collaborative Innovation Networks* by Peter Gloor[50] and *The 7 Habits of Highly Effective People* by Stephen Covey.[51])

Collaboration is the idea of multiple individuals or forces working together for a common goal. One expert on this subject boldly states that by openly sharing ideas and work, the output is exponentially more than the sum of the outputs of all of the individuals working alone.[52] The preacher in Ecclesiastes 4:12 puts it this way, *"Though one may be overpowered, two can defend themselves. A cord of three strands is not quickly broken."* The point here is this – there's strength in working together.

I have often wondered why we don't apply this principle to the Christian family and the church. It seems as if both institutions are trying to do the same thing – develop spiritually mature young people who go on for God (see Ephesians 6:4 and Ephesians 4:14-15). You see, there is our common goal. We want the next generation to go on living for God. It only makes sense that if the two institutions (the home and the church) would work together, the outcome would be greater. In the words of Reggie Joiner, "What if the church and the home combined their efforts and began to work off the same page for the sake of the children? We propose…the potentially revolutionary effect that a true merger between the church and the home could have on the lives of children."[53]

Biblical Examples

Let's start our discussion of this idea of intentional collaboration between the family and the church by looking at two examples from the New Testament where this concept actually worked.

The Example of John Mark

The church was young and it was already facing severe persecution from a military and political regime that had martyred James, one of the Apostles (see Acts 12:1-19). On this particular night in the story, the corrupt ruler King Herod had also imprisoned Peter with the probable intent to martyr him as well. Not knowing what else to do, the early church gathered in a home prayer meeting to call out to God, and here is where we are introduced to young John Mark. That fervent, all-night prayer meeting was held in his mother Mary's home (v. 12). Undoubtedly this young man grew up in church and was a keen eye witness to the functions of this zealous and passionate home-based church. Yes, John Mark grew up in a Christian home and he most certainly was a church kid. He had the unique privilege of seeing firsthand the miracle of Peter's release from prison and his delivery from the clutches of King Herod.

I am certain that his upbringing in a consistent, Christian family and his own personal involvement in the church helped to shape and mold him into a fine young man. I make this observation because in just a short period of time in the chronology of Acts, the early church commissioned and sent out the very first team of missionaries – and, to his credit, John Mark was a part of that team.

It is significant to note again here that a student (John Mark) went along on this first short-term missions trip. Today, centuries later, the phenomenon of taking young people on missions trips has developed into a fairly large industry. According to a well-known evangelical magazine, millions of teenagers go on short-term missions trips each year,[54] and sociologist and author Christian Smith reports that almost one-third of all American high school students have participated in "missions or service" trips.[55] John Mark went along on this first missions endeavor. It seemed as if this young man was on the fast-track of success as a Godly young man. But, as I mentioned earlier, he faced some very serious bumps along the way (See Chapter 3). Acts 13:13 tells how he bailed; he quit the team and went back home. This departure from the trip ultimately cased a serious division between the team leaders, Barnabas and Saul (soon to be called the Apostle Paul). The last paragraph of Acts 15 (verses 36-41) informs us about what happened next. The team split up and Barnabas took John Mark to Cyprus, and Paul took another young man, Silas, and headed out to Syria and Cilicia.

As radio commentator and oft-quoted Paul Harvey used to say, here's *the rest of the story*. John Mark did not end up a quitter or a failure – quite the contrary. He was greatly used of God to pen the Gospel of Mark and he ultimately received high praise from the veteran, now-aged Paul in 2 Timothy 4:11, "...*he is helpful to me in my ministry.*" This *failure* became useful and profitable.

John Mark was a very real example of a young man who grew up surrounded by the secure fences of both a Godly family and a local church.

The Example of Timothy

The setting for our next Biblical example now switches to Lystra, a city in Asia Minor, which would be in the modern-day country of Turkey. There Paul meets another church kid, Timothy. Although he grew up with some cultural and perhaps spiritual dysfunction in his family, Timothy also matured under the influence of a Godly mother and grandmother. (See 2 Timothy 1:5 for a description of the genuine faith that was found from generation to generation in this family.)

This young man too had a promising future. He had a solid reputation in the church and was willing to make a personal and culturally-sensitive commitment in order to have a more effective ministry.

As I highlighted before in the example of John Mark, this student, Timothy was also an active participant in one of the church's earliest missions trips. He accompanied Paul and Silas and endeared himself to both of them as they witnessed the growth and expansion of the early church. Timothy was considered faithful and dependable (1 Corinthians 4:17) and the Lord used him as a strategic part of the early missions endeavors.

Bible scholars observe that perhaps he was rather timid and fearful (2 Timothy 1:7), and maybe somewhat sickly (1 Timothy 5:23). Yet, he too was someone who went on to be greatly used of God. He served as a pastor in the great cross-cultural city of Ephesus and was the recipient of two of Paul's very personal and practical letters – 1 and 2 Timothy.

There are two noteworthy passages in the Epistles to Timothy that contain important and practical inter-generational challenges. The first is found in 1 Timothy 4:12: *"Don't let anyone look down on you because you are young, but set an example for the believers in speech, in life, in love, in faith, and in purity."* We'll look at this verse again later on, but for our purposes now, please note that Paul expected his student to be an example to other believers of other ages in the church. What an encouragement this can be for today's youth! I've had the opportunity during my years in youth ministry to have seen this happen over and over again. Young people actively living for God and enthusiastically serving Him will always be a positive example to other age groups.

The other essential inter-generational challenge in these letters is in the verse I mentioned earlier in our discussion about Timothy's mother and grandmother – 2 Timothy 1:5: *"I have been reminded of your sincere faith, which first lived in your grandmother Lois and in your mother Eunice and, I am persuaded, now lives in you also."* Be sure to notice the genuine, sincere, or consistent faith that was demonstrated in the lives of Timothy's ancestors. (Actually, I love the language that is used in this verse in the King James Version – *"unfeigned faith,"* a term that means authentic or "un-faked.") But, there is an emphasis in this verse that is imperative to consider. Twice in verse 5, Paul points out the sincere, genuine, or real faith that Timothy himself possessed. Sure, we can honor his mom and grandmother for their authentic faith, but twice in this one verse Timothy is commended for his genuine faith. Three generations are listed here, but it is the third generation (Timothy) that is applauded for his consistent walk with God. This is a faith that was translated and reproduced from generation to generation.

Timothy is a great example of a church kid from a consistent Christian home (at least from the influence of his mother and grandmother) who also grew up to walk with God and who had a lasting inter-generational ministry and impact as recorded in God's Word (2 Timothy 2:2).

Practical Suggestions for a Powerful Parent and Church Collaborative Impact

Yes, it's a powerful influence when the home and the church work together for the common goal of developing lasting spiritual maturity in the lives of the next generation. But, let's face it – the church and parents aren't often on the same page. According to a past president of Young Life, only 15 to 20 percent of American teenagers are significantly involved in a local church.[56] Likewise, in Ken Ham's book *Already Gone*, he reports that almost 90% of today's current young adults actually checked out of local church involvement during their middle school and high school years.[57]

I admit that some of these statistics can be explained away. Maybe some of those surveyed by Young Life were never actively involved in church, and maybe some of Ham's respondents were raised in inconsistent Christian homes. But, we can't shake the catastrophic numbers. The family and the church are not working together in most traditional churches today. In my own personal experience as a speaker and writer, I have talked to several people on each side of the issue who are blaming the other institution for this departure from the faith. I have met some perhaps well-meaning, but confused Christians parents who are keeping their kids out of church youth programs because they feel that they are the only ones who can truly influence their children. I have also met many church leaders who blame parents for not making the commitment to keep their kids active in church.

Friends, please hear me on this point. I firmly believe that parents have the ultimate Biblical authority to raise their children (Proverbs 22:6). I also believe that this basic truth includes the parental responsibility to train and educate their kids (Deuteronomy 6 and Psalm 1:1). Even though my wife and I chose to put our kids in public schools, we firmly believe it is our responsibility to train our children – not the government's. (See my historical perspective on compulsory education in the United States in Chapter 1 of this book.) We made the commitment to do all we could do to be involved in the education of our children, including our involvement as parents in the schools our kids attended. However, I have talked to some homeschooling parents who are not allowing their children to be involved in church youth meetings or activities. I certainly champion their commitment to educate their own children, but I also question their motives for keeping their kids out of church youth group. Parents, our kids need the church! The church is God's plan for this age – and a collaborative effort between the home and the church will have a potent and lasting influence on the coming generation.

I have spent over 35 years of my life involved in local church youth ministry. I love youth pastors and have spent most of my ministry training and encouraging them in their strategic ministries with teens. But, to be honest with you, I have some blunt, but candid words for them, too. Many youth workers are blaming parents for the spiritual immaturity they are seeing in the lives of the teenagers in their groups. This accusation has developed over the recent trend of busy kids. I surveyed around 400 youth workers a couple of years ago and asked them what their biggest concerns in youth ministry were. The top two answers were busy kids and parents of teenagers. So many youth workers are seeing a lack of commitment on the part of teens (and ultimately parents, of course) to Sunday school, church services, youth group meetings, youth group activities, and summer events. It seems as if this generation of young people is overly involved in school, homework, work, sports, band, choir, yearbook, and many other *good* things, so that they cannot be involved in the church youth group. Many youth pastors feel that parents seem to be more concerned and involved with their kids' other activities than they are in keeping their kids in church. Yet, I wonder if this frustration is linked more to their personal feelings of insecurity over the external success of their programming than it is to their genuine desire for spiritual growth in the lives of individual students. In other words, some may be more worried about *their* schedule or program than they are about individual spiritual maturity. That's exactly why these two groups must work together.

So, this issue has two sides to it. I can see the strengths and the weaknesses of both opinions. Some parents blame the church for carnality and for separating children from their parents, and some youth workers accuse parents of not making a commitment to the church youth program.

I want to take the opportunity now to give some loving and heartfelt advice to both church leaders and to parents about the collaborative strength that comes from the family and the church working together to help develop spiritual maturity in the lives of our kids.

Advice for Church Leaders: Equip parents to be a spiritual success with their own children.

It saddens me to think that the traditional church today has lost its focus – and, to be honest with you, I'm making that indictment of mega-churches and smaller conventional churches alike. I have had the occasion recently to visit some of this nation's most popular mega-churches. Their facilities, their programs, their staffing, and their services are absolutely incredible. I've also spent several Sundays over the past few years preaching in some of this country's "average" churches. (According the Hartford Institute, the average church in the United States has 75 attendees.) Frankly, it's been hard to see a genuine "equipping" ministry in action anywhere. It's not that churches don't do it, but I'm not sure it's their focus.

Ephesians 4:12 is very clear. Church leaders are gifted by God to prepare, perfect, or equip God's people for *"works of service."* That is to be the focus of the mission of the church. Churches are designed by God to build people toward spiritual maturity and pastors are to equip those maturing people to actively serve Him in and through the local church.

This familiar passage then is the foundation for this initial piece of advice for church leaders. Churches must equip parents to be a spiritual success with their kids. Parenting is one of the most important things we will ever do. It is how we pass our legacy of faith and truth down the line to future generations. That's why it is so essential for youth pastors, youth workers, and other church leaders to equip parents for parenting.

Youth ministry is really a ministry to parents. I have heard veteran youth worker Dewey Bertolini say, "Our ultimate effectiveness with teenagers may depend upon our concerted effort to gain an influence in the homes of our youth." Sure, youth workers can have a real impact on the lives of impressionable youth, but our most effective long-term ministry may indeed be our entrance into the lives and hearts of parents. We understand that God's Word gives the ultimate responsibility of raising children to parents. That's why the focus of local church youth ministry should be upon equipping parents to be effective in how they raise their kids for the glory of God. However, most youth workers spend the majority of their time ministering to teenagers. The problem is that we sometimes fail to implement even the basic ingredients of an equipping ministry to the people most responsible for the spiritual maturity of our students: their parents.

The Lord has given my wife and me the opportunity to lead several seminars and workshops over the past few years for parents of teenagers and preteens (This only means that "we're old"; our kids are grown). This experience has convinced us that many parents are looking for the following five things from the church: communication, training, fellowship, encouragement and support, and resources. We have talked to hundreds of parents of teenagers and preteens in churches of various sizes all across the country. These interviews give ample credence to our belief that every church should include these five priorities in an equipping ministry to parents.

I sincerely encourage all youth pastors and youth workers (and all church leaders for that matter) to figure out how these five elements can fit into their ministries. Here's the key question: how can your church "equip" or "prepare" parents by utilizing these five areas? Obviously this process must begin early. I'm sure that no one is really ever prepared to be a parent. But, church leaders can work hard to incorporate an equipping philosophy into the structure and programming of their ministries.

It's also important to note that church leaders shouldn't be critical of parents that do not support the church's programs or schedule. Instead, the church should do everything it can to support parents and help them be spiritual successes with their kids. I am convinced that churches of any size will be much more effective, and have less frustrated leaders, by making this equipping ministry the focus of how the church operates.

Advice for Parents: Make church and youth group a top priority for you and your family.

I grew up in church, served for several years on a church staff, and have been active in churches all of my life, and so has my wife. Our children are all serving the Lord in vocational ministry and we're already praying specifically for our grand-children, that they too will grow up to love the church and the work Christ is doing through the church in this age. I can honestly say that I love the church. I know that I mentioned above that there are things about today's church that sadden and frustrate me. I sense that in some cases the contemporary church has become somewhat irrelevant in today's postmodern culture. Yet (I am trying to adequately express my true feelings at this point), I am personally grieved by the attitude expressed by many today who are willfully walking away from the church. I don't believe we have that choice.

Christ died for His church (Ephesians 5:15-27), the church is His body (Colossians 1:18), and the church is His bride (Ephesians 5:25 and Revelation 19:7). It doesn't make sense for us to be critical or negative about His church. Instead, let's search the Scriptures and refocus our ministries on how Christ intended His church to function.

This brings me to my practical advice for parents. I base this advice squarely upon the Word of God, my own personal experience as a parent, and my many years of involvement in church youth ministry.

Please make church a priority for you and your kids! I want to share this counsel across the whole spectrum of various Christian parenting philosophies and attitudes. If you are a parent who has the idea that outside activities (such as a part-time job, homework, or sports, etc.) are more important for your kids than regular church involvement, or if you are a committed homeschool parent who has come to the conclusion that you are the only proper influence on your children – I plead with you. Keep your kids in church.

My perspective here needs to be kept in balance. I was a high school and college basketball player, and I understand the value of athletics. Our children had to work part-time jobs to have spending money and to pay for college. Plus, I have already stated in this book that I believe parents have the responsibility to train their own children. So, I ask you not to miss what I am saying.

Children must learn very early on, and they need to re-learn this idea as they go through their quest for personal independence during the adolescent years, that church is a priority. I'm not just talking here about *attending* church – sitting stoically alongside parents. I'm talking about active *involvement* and dynamic *participation* in the local church. (We'll talk more about the idea of church involvement and participation later on in the book.)

There are several reasons why I am so emphatic about local church involvement for parents and their kids. The main reason, which I've already mentioned above, is this - Christ wants us to love His church and God's Word instructs us to be involved in church (Ephesians 4:11-16, Hebrews 10:25, 1 Corinthians 12, and Romans 12:3-8).

Parents also have the unique opportunity to develop habits or an appetite for what is good and what is right in the lives of their children. I appreciate the principle found in Proverbs 3:27: "Do not withhold good from those who deserve it, when it is in your power to act." I believe the habits of Sunday school attendance and participation in church youth group are good things and should be a part of every Christian young person's life.

One of the reasons I say that is because of the familiar illustration in the Old Testament story of Shadrach, Meshach, and Abednego in Daniel 3. I love the account of how these three Hebrew young men stood together, even when faced with the threat of death by the hands of Nebuchadnezzar. Perhaps you've noticed the fact that these men are always mentioned together. I believe there is a confidence that comes from standing together with good friends. I see this principle vividly illustrated in church youth groups everywhere I go. Today's students need Godly Christian friends. They need to know that there are other Christian young people out there who have the same desire for and commitment to God. This is one reason why I also love and appreciate youth rallies, youth conferences, youth camps, and youth missions trip. Christian kids will meet other Christian kids at places like that who love the Lord and who want to stand up for God, too. The association with other committed Christ-followers is a powerful influence – on all of us!

There is another huge advantage for our young people being involved in church youth ministry and that is the opportunity for our young people to "get out of Dodge" and see that we are serving a big God who is doing big things all around the globe. Each of us tends to get nearsighted and provincial if we're not careful. I've had the opportunity to minister annually in some of this country's largest inner cities. Even in large cities with millions of people nearby, it is very easy to get stuck in your own neighborhood. That's why we need an intentional strategy like what is found in Acts 1:8: *"But you will receive power when the Holy Spirit comes on you; and you will be my witnesses in Jerusalem, and in all Judea and Samaria, and to the ends of the earth."* God wants us all to reach out in a strategy of concentric circles until we have a world-wide impact.

Parents, our kids need to see how big our God is. They need to see how other Christian families and how other church youth groups function. One of the grandest blessings of my life has been to travel internationally and have the privilege to see brothers and sisters in Christ worshiping Him in so many different ways. See, that kind of thing happens in youth groups: my children meet your children, they have the opportunity to hang out with other Christian kids, they participate in youth ministry events where they meet even more Christians, and then they learn to reach out and minister to more and more believers all around this globe. They can learn the importance of the worldwide body of Christ from the Scriptures certainly, but the reinforcement of experiencing it on their own is a powerful demonstration of just how big our God is.

Our kids need the church.

Further Advice for Collaborative Influence: Families should make the commitment to be involved in church together.

It doesn't matter if you attend a traditional church, a mega church, an average church, a house church, a simple church,[58] or a "family-integrated"[59] church – the important thing about this principle of collaboration is the need to blend the Christian home and the church together into one stronger influence upon the lives of the next generation. That's why I strongly encourage church leaders and Christian parents alike to make the commitment for families to be involved in the church together.

Some pastors, youth pastors, and other church leaders may need a paradigm shift in the way they have thought about basic church ministry to provide or create opportunities for families to be involved in some select church functions together. Parents may also need to look at church involvement differently as well. Instead of viewing the church with a consumer mindset of "what does the church offer me?" look at it from a serving model with the attitude of "what can we do to serve Christ in the church?" With the Biblical instruction about gifts and gifted-ness in mind (see Ephesians 4:11-6, Romans 12:3-8, and 1 Corin-thians 12), parents should do everything they can to model a dedication and loyalty to the church by involving their family in specific ways over the long haul. I am not saying that a family's involvement in church should turn into a guilt-motivated, come to church every-time-the-door-is-open mentality. That's not it. As a parent of grown children and as a long-time youth worker, I definitely encourage parents to be consistent in the specific in-volvements they select for their family. This suggestion is not meant, however, to be a license to allow parents to handpick only the church services or functions they want to attend. Par-ents will need to find the balance here that works for their fam-ily.

The key is that we must remember Paul's admonition in Colossians 1:18: "*And he is the head of the body, the church; he is the beginning and the firstborn from among the dead, so that in everything he might have the supremacy.*" Christ is the "*head of the church*" and as our Lord and Savior, He deserves and demands "*supremacy*" or the "*preeminence*" (KJV). I believe that there is a very clear ap-plication of this point – if Christ is indeed the top priority in our lives and if our goal is to please Him, then His church will also be the key ingredient of our lives and of our families. It doesn't work to love Christ and have a dedication to Him, and then not make a commitment to His church!

I'll end this chapter on a personal note. My wife and I made a decision before the Lord, early on in the life of our fam-ily, that our involvement in church would be a major priority for us. To be direct with you, we did not raise our kids with a "we have to go to everything" mindset. Yet, we did commit as a fam-ily to the following five basic church-life functions: (1) the faith-ful communication of God's Word (preaching and teaching) – we wanted our children to grow up with a love for the clear, complete, and creative preaching of Scripture; (2) worship and prayer – even though I am not a musician, we tried to build an appreciation in our children for God-honoring and enthusiastic musical expressions of worship to the Lord; (3) service and out-reach – my wife and I modeled a personal involvement in various ministries of our churches where we could serve the Lord in our own areas of giftedness, plus we did our best to develop ways we could serve Him *together* in the church; (4) giving – we made financial giving and tithing to the church a significant part of our budget and encouraged our children to do that as well; and (5) fellowship – we made fellowship with God's people of all ages (peer ministry and inter-generational ministry) and hospitality in our home an essential component of our family's schedule and resources. (We'll revisit these 5 personal commitments later on in the book.)

The collaborative effort of families and the church working together for the same purpose is a powerful, life-changing influence. Both institutions want our kids to come to Christ and to follow Him as adults. Maybe it does *take a church*. We'll take a look at how this works in the next chapter.

Chapter Five: "Entrust to Reliable Men"
Building an Inter-Generational Church

From Jerusalem, to Antioch, to Ephesus, to Corinth – each New Testament church was different. There are no cookie-cutter churches in the Bible. The early Jerusalem church had all things in common. The Antioch church was the first church to send out missionaries. Some churches obviously met in homes, while others seemed to gather in public buildings. Some were commended for their spiritual growth and vitality; others were criticized for their carnality and lack of growth. Yet, each church mentioned in the pages of Scripture existed for the same purpose – to produce spiritually mature believers (Ephesians 4:11-16). (See Chapter 3 for further discussion on the purpose of the church.)

It saddens me somewhat to think that the traditional church in today's culture has become quite predictable and repetitious. Sure, some churches meet in warehouses, strip malls, and outdoor pavilions. Others divide into small groups and some emphasize expository preaching. Typical churches average less than 100 people,[60] while attendance in this country's largest churches is growing significantly[61] (including a handful of individual churches that average around 20,000 people[62]). I'm sure that most contemporary church leaders, in smaller churches and in mega-churches alike, would tout their own desire to fulfill the church's mission to develop fully-devoted followers of Christ. However, the basic methodology and structure in seeking to accomplish this purpose has become all too pedestrian and conventional.

I'm talking here, of course, about the relatively recent development of segregating generations. One author, who criticizes the propensity to divide congregations by age group, says that "these new methods [of age segregation] were conceived to reach young people more effectively and grow churches. Because of the initial increase in church attendance, the widespread reception, and the years of practice, these methods are now accepted as a necessary part of church life."[63]

Another writer makes this observation: "The field of youth ministry exists because churches recognized that adolescence was a unique phase of development (or at least they knew teenagers were different). With good intentions and recognizing that teenagers needed special attention, churches began segregating teens to their own classrooms away from the adults and children, and they hired individuals whose specific job it was to spend time with teenagers." The author continues, adding, "Before long, age-specific programming became the norm not just on Sunday mornings, but throughout the life of the church. On one hand, this makes sense – yet it has fueled a great deal of dysfunction."[64]

It's imperative that the church not throw out its Biblical mission in an attempt to change methodologies. Perhaps the exclusive separation of various age groups in the church was originally done out of pure motives and a sincere desire to reach and minister to the various generations. However, what began as a desire to be relevant and effective may have gradually morphed into classic traditionalism. The point is, no matter what the church looks like, the God-given purpose of the church is to *equip* (Ephesians 4:11-16) His people to grow toward maturity in Christ. What we want from all generations is for believers to go on living for Him over the long haul of life.

I am absolutely convinced that this process works best in an inter-generational community of Christ-followers who are committed to the body and who desperately want to help other believers grow in Christ and go on living for Him. Is there a way for churches to become truly inter-generational in mission and function? It is my contention that a call for balance is in order. I believe in the merits of peer ministry and have already argued for making a commitment for reaching the next generation a top priority in the church. (I'll also present some practical advantages of local church youth ministry in Chapter 7.) *How* we make that commitment now comes into question. What is a Biblical and the most effective way churches can reach and minister to future generations? We'll take a look at some various ways churches have structured their programs and then consider the balance of peer, age-group ministries alongside of a genuine and lasting inter-generational ministry.

One-Generational Programming

It seems that many churches are mostly *one-generational* in the way their ministries and church functions are organized. The children meet in one area of the building, the teenagers meet in another, and the adults gather in still another section. This age-segregated style of ministry often spreads out throughout the various educational programs of the church and usually includes a lineup of Sunday school, church-time

"children's church," and Vacation Bible School. This approach habitually extends throughout the entire maturing stages of human growth and development and sometimes even includes young adult programming that isolates emerging generations from the adult ministries of the church. (The *young church*[65] movement that gained quite a following a few years ago is an example of the philosophy that isolates college age or singles from other groups of adults. Mars Hill Bible Church near Grand Rapids, Michigan, popularized by its former preaching pastor, Rob Bell, is a specific illustration of a local church that came into existence through the efforts of an existing church to host age-specific, one-generational services.[66]) Youth ministry researcher Kara Powell of Fuller Seminary's "Youth Institute" puts it this way, "In churches today, there's an adult worship service and a youth worship service. We have an adult worship team and a teen worship band. The larger the church, the greater the separation."[67] Many traditional churches break the age groups down even more by dividing their adult educational functions into smaller classes segregated by age or various life stages.

Of course, pastors and other church leaders have some rationale for this approach to ministry. As presented earlier in this book, age-segregated thinking has become the traditional norm for the church and hence it seems to make sense to keep it that way. In addition, pastors, Christian education directors, and Sunday school teachers understand that each separate age group learns and behaves differently than other age groups. Educationally speaking, it is usually not effective to have children, youth, and adults in the same room. Children learn at one level, teenagers at another level, and adults at another. There is a great deal of merit for dividing the generations for educational purposes. 1 Corinthians 13:11 advocates this idea this way, *"When I was a child, I talked like a child, I thought like a child, I reasoned like a child. When I became a man, I put childish ways behind me."* (Practical advantages of an age-segregated approach will be discussed later on in this book.) Simply put, children, youth, and adults are different; and it makes sense to develop ministries that treat them differently.

However, if churches separate people by age only, I believe they are making a big mistake. The various generations need each other and the church must be intentional and proactive about making wholesome, genuine, and lasting intergenerational connections.

Multi-Generational Programming

Many churches host what I call *multi-generational* programs – where members of various generations meet together, but have very little interaction or connection with each other.

Typical Sunday morning worship services often fit into this category. Children sometimes accompany their parents, teenagers congregate with other teenagers, and a mixture of adults all meet together for times of worship

Multi-Generational Ministries

✓ Age-groups meet alongside each other, but very little interaction

Children   **Youth**   **Adults**

and preaching. However, the assorted age groups hardly ever connect and very seldom develop close relationships with each other.

We've all seen this happen, of course – whether during potluck suppers or church business meetings. The generations in these church gatherings are all present together in the same room, but they have very little contact with the members of other generations.

Somehow church leaders are quick to reveal their complicity with this strategy as well. So many churches today are characterized by a *one-generational* or *multi-generational* approach. The generations are mostly isolated from each other, and when we do gather the various generations together, we do so without a clear, purposeful plan for developing growing and loving inter-generational relationships. Yet, we wouldn't allow this segregation in any other aspect of our ministries. We'd want members of different races or ethnic groups to connect with each other, and we'd want people from various economic classes to get to know each other. However, we seem perfectly fine allowing different generations to be alienated from each other.

This generational separation seems opposed to the Biblical model of the church as presented in Paul's Epistle to the Ephesians – especially in Chapter 4's teaching on the unity of the "body of Christ." It's obvious in the pages of Scripture that Christ intended His body to be unified racially, economically, and generationally. That's why it is imperative that local churches are intentional about fostering and nurturing inter-generational relationships.

Inter-Generational Programming

It's time to develop a calculated and deliberate plan to build positive and growing *inter-generational* connections in the church. In spite of the "generation gap" that has grown in ever-widening measures in the church and in Western culture, it is crucial that we take this matter seriously in the church. Our kids are leaving the church and one reason they are dropping out after high school is that

they do not have strong relationships with very many adults. Let's face it. Traditional churches have isolated youth from adults throughout their developmental years. In many churches, the only adults teenagers know are their parents and perhaps a handful of adult youth workers.

A few years ago I heard well-known youth ministry expert Dr. Chap Clark say that in order for a high school graduate to stay plugged into the church following graduation from high school, he or she needs strong relationships with five significant adults other than their parents. (Clark's statistic has been quoted in several publications recently, including by his Fuller Seminary colleague Kara Powell in her article *Moving Away from the Kid's Table* on the Fuller web site at: http://fulleryouthinstitute.org/2010/08/moving-away-from-the-kid-table/.)

Clark's point makes sense. We must help our young people develop growing relationships with older people in the church. It doesn't make sense and it is not effective to separate the church along generational lines exclusively. The various generations need each other. Youth need the maturity and wisdom of older people and the older generations need the energy, vitality, and idealism of younger people. Church leaders would be wise to help the members of different generations to connect with each other – and I highly recommend that these connections start with the older adults. Let's not assume that our children and youth will have the confidence or initiative to approach adults with the motive of building growing relationships with them.

As mentioned above, these inter-generational connections must be intentional and deliberate. As Clark points out, "In most churches, when adolescents leave high school, there are few programmatic options available for them much less a welcoming community that has committed to bring them into the life of the body."[68] I'm wondering if very many churches have intentional plans to welcome young people into the overall life of the church. Here are some simple suggestions that any church can implement to help emerging generations actually feel welcome in the overall body.

How to Build Inter-Generational Connections in Your Church
1. Motivate and train adults to pray **FOR** emerging generations.

One of the best ways to help your church develop a burden for youth is to encourage the older adults to pray intentionally and specifically for them – by name. It's really very simple. Start by compiling a list of your church's teenagers. Then meet with your church's older adults. Ask them to pray for the teenagers by name. Remind them how important it is for them to pray for the church's youth. You could divide your list of names by each day of the week or assign specific students as prayer partners with specific adults. I know of one church that actually makes prayer cards, like conventional baseball cards, for each student. The important thing is to do everything you can to motivate the adults to pray specifically for individual young people. Once they begin to pray regularly and intentionally for the teenagers, the Lord will put a growing burden on their hearts for those students to live for God. You'll be amazed at how much this helps.

2. <u>Give your adults specific opportunities to **SEE** younger generations actively living for the Lord</u>.
I am a big fan of connecting the generations in church. The Apostle Paul must have wanted that to happen, too. He wrote this in 1 Timothy 4:12, *"Don't let anyone look down on you because you are young, but set an example for the believers."* Being an example requires exposure. Separating the generations does not give them any exposure to each other. I am convinced that the older generations want the same thing you do – for your church's young people to live for God! So, do whatever you can to give the older generations specific opportunities to see positive examples of your students living for the Lord and serving Him. Perhaps the traditional "youth night" serv-

ices are one way of doing that. But, there are other tangible ways as well. Give your teens specific and visible opportunities to serve the Lord in the church. For example, you could schedule work days for the students to invest in "sweat equity" in the church.

Tim Ahlgrim, one of my colleagues at Vision For Youth, had a great idea. When he was a youth pastor, he actually taught the senior citizens' Sunday school class. On several occasions he took them on a "field trip" to the youth class where they could see and hear the youth worship the Lord with fervency, enthusiasm, and authenticity. The seniors were also there to hear the announcements and the testimonies of the many, many ways the youth group served the Lord and actively witnessed for Him. This simple activity gave the senior adults a glimpse into the teenage world of genuine passion and zeal for the things of Christ.

This may sound somewhat idealistic, and we will discuss this topic more later on in the book, but I am certain that down deep in their hearts, the various generations of true believers want the same thing – the opportunity to worship the Lord in *"spirit and in truth"* (John 4:23). Externals and tastes change across the spectrum of generational differences, but there will never be unity or camaraderie between the generations until both groups actually have the opportunity to see each other in action.

3. Provide specific opportunities for the different generations to have interaction and fellowship **WITH EACH OTHER**.

Let's face it; most of our churches do not give the various generations even simple opportunities to get to know each other. Why not schedule and plan a simple fellowship time for your church's teenagers and older adults? Some churches ask their youth to put on a meal for the seniors. Other churches schedule a table-game night at the church. The actual ideas are almost endless. The important thing is for the youth and the older adults to get to know each other. You'll be amazed at how positive and beneficial this simple idea can be.

Another way for the generations to get to know each other is to encourage older generations to tell their stories, or their testimonies, to younger generations. Today's young people love stories. They respond very well to the real-life accounts of mature, older Christians who can share the stories of how God led them through the ups and downs of a lifetime of living for Christ. It is amazing to think how God can and will use older believers to encourage and help young people who are going through some of the very things they went through. The Apostle Paul shares this idea in 2 Corinthians 1:3-7. Here's what he says in verse 6, *"If we are distressed, it is for your comfort and salvation; if we are comforted, it is for your comfort, which produces in you patient endurance of the same sufferings we suffer."*

4. Develop **INTENTIONAL INTER-GENERATIONAL MENTORING** connections.
    One of the best ways to institute healthy and growing inter-generational relationships is through an intentional and planned church-based mentoring ministry. Much is being said and written today about the

idea of mentoring. A recent Google search revealed over 42 million websites on the subject. True inter-generational mentoring provides another positive layer of caring and committed adults who are willing to spend time with young people in the development of maturing interpersonal relationships. (Much more material about how to develop and institute a church-based mentoring initiative will be presented in Chapter 11 of this book.)

5. <u>Begin to provide ways for different generations to pray **WITH** each other</u>.
    It will probably be threatening to schedule prayer times together as the first way to connect the genera-tions. Serious prayer times should be intimate and can be intimidating if relationships are not built first. However, once the various generations have prayed *for* each other and once they get to know each other, praying together can be a powerful connecting influ-ence. True inter-generational prayer services can be very positive for any church, but be sure to give these prayer sessions the time to develop into something truly interactive and intimate. I still fondly remember the times as a young boy that I went with my parents to our church's Wednesday evening prayer meetings. I'll never forget hearing the older saints pray aloud in those sessions. Those people prayed like God was right there in the room. I'll always remember their passion, their seriousness about prayer, and their de-sire to talk to God. On the other hand, in my years of working with teenagers, I've always valued the prayers of Godly teenagers who too cried out to Him with passion, energy, and a yearning to commune with God. Here's the point – the generations need

each other and prayer is one incredibly valuable way the various generations can connect.

6. Provide significant ways for younger generations to **SERVE ALONGSIDE** older people in established ministries.

The ideal would be to encourage every adult in your church to recruit a younger person to serve alongside them in specific ministry responsibilities. This should be the norm in your church. If someone teaches a VBS class, they should be expected to find a younger person to serve as their assistant. Your sound room staff should be training younger people to someday replace them. Why not ask your church ushers to include young people on the team? And don't forget the worship team. It would be a significant visual aid for the entire church to see older people and younger people serving the Lord together in your church's public music ministry. Church work days can be another opportunity for significant inter-generational relationships to develop. The important thing is to provide or create ways for the different generations to serve the Lord together.

7. Recruit a team of encouraging and loving adults to **ACTIVELY WELCOME EMERGING GENERA-TIONS** (graduating high school seniors and young adults) into the life of the church.

Let's go back to Chap Clark's words I used previously. Churches must develop a "welcoming community that is committed to bring them into the life of the body."[69] Traditionally we kick kids out of youth group when they graduate from high school and then let them flounder trying to transition into the adult world of church. Other churches develop a plan to extend the transition to adulthood by instituting college and career age or young adult ministries that are often also isolated from the overall life of the church. But, no matter when the transition to the adult ministries is made, it is imperative for the church to set up a plan to welcome these emerging young adults into the adult ministries of Sunday school, adult Bible fellowships, or small group ministries.

Calling for a Balanced Approach

There's another way to structure church programs that must be considered, and that is the implementation of a genuine balance between peer ministries, which tend to segregate people by age or sociological groupings for educational and discipleship purposes, and an inter-generational approach, where churches work hard to develop growing and lasting connections between the generations.

There is a movement in some ecclesiastical circles today to totally eliminate age-segregated programming in church.[70] Some recommend the abolition of the Sunday school entirely and point to the secular and humanistic roots of the age-segregated programming in the church in favor of a "Family-Integrated Church." Some of the most vocal lead-

ers of this group, who are also advocating the elimination of church youth ministry, are speakers and writers, such as Voddie Baucham, the author of *Family-Driven Faith,*[71] and Scott Brown, the author of *A Weed in the Church,*[72] and the leading voice of the *National Center for Family-Integrated Churches* organization in Wake Forest, North Carolina.

Without launching into a full expositional treatise here to fully develop these arguments, let it suffice to say that I believe there is a wealth of Biblical support for age-based ministries in the church that allow for God's people to grow and mature according to the way God created them – from physical birth, through childhood, puberty, and throughout the maturing years as aging adults. The following chart identifies some of the basic Biblical principles I use for the establishment of age-based, maturing ministries.

BIBLICAL PRINCIPLES FOR AGE MATURITY
(In Other Words, Do Different Ages Learn at the Same Level of Maturity?)

REFERENCE	BASIC TEXT	PRINCIPLE
1 Corinthians 13:11	"When I was a child, I talked like a child, I thought like a child, I reasoned like a child. When I became a man, I put childish ways behind me."	There is a difference between the way children think and learn and the way adults think and learn.
Ephesians 4:14-15	"Then we will no longer be infants, tossed back and forth by the waves, and blown here and there by every wind of teaching and by the cunning and craftiness of men in their deceitful scheming. Instead, speaking the truth in love, we will in all things grow up into Him."	Children need to be grounded and established in the faith – in a context of church ministry.
2 Timothy 3:10-17	"You, however, know all about my teaching, my way of life... But as for you, continue in what you have learned and have become convinced of, because you know those from whom you learned it, and how from infancy you have known the holy Scriptures."	Parents AND Godly, influential adults can work together to help maturing young people grow in Christ.
2 Timothy 2:2	"And the things you have heard me say in the presence of many witnesses entrust to reliable men who will also be qualified to teach others also."	Paul discipled a younger man, Timothy - who was instructed to keep this process going.
Luke 2:52	"And Jesus grew in wisdom and stature, and in favor with God and men."	Christ Himself went through a maturing process from childhood, through His teenage years, into adulthood.
Psalm 78:1-8	"Will not hide them from their children: we will tell the next generation the praiseworthy deeds of the Lord, His power, and the wonders He has done... So the next generation would know them, even the children yet to be born, and they in turn would tell their children."	There seems to be an educational collaboration between fathers AND other spiritual leaders for the spiritual growth of the next generation.

I believe that the key is a balance of programming and ministries in the church. Some age-appropriate peer ministry seems to be in order and certainly gives the church the opportunity to minister to and reach out to families with children and teenagers, as well as to un-churched community young people who may or may not have spiritually strong parents. However, if we exclusively isolate the generations from the larger scope of other age groups, I believe we are making a big mistake – one that may ultimately lead to a wide-scale departure from the church once kids become adults. A balanced cross-section of ministry programs is essential. This allows children and youth to learn and apply Biblical truth at an appropriate level and gives other age groups, like sub-groupings of adults, the opportunity to learn and grow within basic sociological settings. This balance also allows the church to formulate and institute some of the above mentioned suggestions for making inter-generational connections. In other words, it is important to schedule some age-specific ministries (like Sunday school and youth ministry), but also balance those ministries with intentional mentoring (see Chapter 11) and other specific inter-generational ministries.

Earlier in this book (see Chapter 4) I identified five basic church-life functions: communication of God's Word, worship and prayer, service and outreach, giving, and fellowship. My wife and I made the commitment in our family to be actively involved in these five priorities as our children grew up. We came to the conclusion that these five basic programming functions would be the essential ingredients of our family's involvement in the church we attended. I wholeheartedly believe that each of these five ingredients of church life can and should feature a balance of one-generational programming, multi-generational programming, and inter-generational ministry.

For example, a truly inter-generational church will feature a balance of various ministries that communicate the Bible. Certainly this will comprise one-generational ministries such as

Sunday school and youth ministry where church people meet almost exclusively in age groups to study the Scriptures, and it will include multi-generational aspects such as weekend worship services where different generations gather together. Furthermore, it will also incorporate inter-generational Bible studies such as a small group ministry where members of the various generations truly connect. Here's another example using another of the above listed church-life functions. An inter-generational church will also include balanced venues of fellowship – like youth group socials where Christian kids, for example, can meet and hang out with other Christian kids. It will also host multi-generational functions, like church dinners, where members of all generations can assemble together, and these churches will also make a commitment to host intentional inter-generational events where the different generations can actually develop true Biblical fellowship and church unity.

The following chart contains a brief list of balanced programming ideas that will give readers an overview of how churches of a wide range of sizes and distinctives can further their journey toward a genuine inter-generational approach.

EXAMPLES OF BALANCED PROGRAMMING IDEAS

CHURCH LIFE FUNCTIONS	ONE GENERATIONAL	MULTI-GENERATIONAL	INTER-GENERATIONAL
1. COMMUNICATION OF GOD'S WORD			
	Sunday School	Preaching Services	Small Group Bible Studies
	Youth Ministry & Children's Ministry	Some Sunday School Classes	1-to-1 Bible Studies
2. WORSHIP & PRAYER			
	Adult-Led Worship Teams	Worship Times in Church Services	Worship Teams (All Ages Involved Together)
	Traditional Adult Prayer Meetings	Sunday School Prayer Campaigns	Inter-Generational Prayer Times (In Groups or Individuals)
3. SERVICE & OUTREACH			
	Evangelism Programs & Classes	Invite Friends to Church	Inter-Generational Evangelistic Opportunities
	Typical Ministry Positions	Church Work Days	Inter-Generational Ministries
4. GIVING			
	Appeals to Adults	Church-Wide Appeals	Encourage All Ages to Give & Tithe
	Offering / Giving Envelopes	Church Stewardship Projects	Inter-Generational Projects
5. FELLOWSHIP			
	Age-Group Socials	Church Dinners	Youth Group / Senior Adult Socials
	Sunday School Class Parties	Other Church Events	Intentional Inter-Generational Activities

As presented throughout this book, the generation gap must be eliminated. Older people need young people, and young people need older people. It's time to institute a balanced approach. The next five chapters will take a look at how specific age group ministries, from children through senior adults, can be truly inter-generational.

Chapter Six: Children's Ministry
"No Longer Children"

Remember when the argument broke out among Christ's disciples over which one of them would be the greatest? (See Luke 9:46-48.) Christ responded by using a child as a visual aid: *"Jesus, knowing their thoughts, took a little child and had him stand beside him. Then he said to them, 'Whoever welcomes this little child in my name welcomes me, and whoever welcomes me welcomes the one who sent me. For he who is least among you all – he is the greatest.'"*

I love how the authors of the book *Sticky Faith: Everyday Ideas to Build Lasting Faith in Your Kids* describe this passage:

An understanding of the Greek phrasing that Jesus uses in this well-known statement about intergenerational relationships makes his words all the more difficult for the disciples to swallow. The Greek verb Jesus uses here for *welcome* is *dechomai* (pronounced 'DECK-oh-my'), which often meant showing hospitality to guests. Thus it carries a certain connotation of servanthood. In the first century, taking care of both guests and children was a task generally fulfilled by members of society who were viewed different from, and even inferior to, the male disciples – meaning women and slaves. Thus Jesus was asking the disciples, who had just been arguing about their individual greatness, to show utmost humility by embracing the kids in their midst. According to Jesus, greatness – and dare we say 'great' parenting and 'great' Christian living – emerges as adults welcome children.[73]

American researcher George Barna reported just a few short years ago that children's ministry "should be your church's number 1 priority," and that children should be the "primary focus" of a church's ministry.[74] Here is his rationale for those broad sweeping statements: "nearly half of all Americans who accept Jesus Christ as their savior do so before reaching the age of 13."[75]

There's more research that substantiates that claim. A few years ago I took a quick survey of several hundred teenagers who were attending a fairly large Christian youth event that was somewhat national in scope. My assessment revealed the following information:

- ✓ Most Christian young people come to Christ as children.
- ✓ Most of them that grew up in Christian homes were led to Christ by their parents.
- ✓ The second highest percentage of those accepting Christ did so through a church or para-church's children's ministry.

Barna agrees, "Most people decide what they will do about Jesus – either wholeheartedly follow, merely acknowledge, or ignore or reject him – while they are young."[76]

A strong children's ministry is indeed a top priority for the church. This book is not, however, intended to be a manual for doing children's ministry. There is a wealth of information and resources available to help church leaders develop a positive and constructive ministry to children. It's also important to note that I am not a specialist or an expert in children's ministry. I have some experience in that field, but I must admit that this is not my area of proficiency. Plus, that is not the focus of this book. Instead this chapter will include principles and suggestions on how to include children's ministry in our overall discussion of developing an inter-generational emphasis in the church.

Characteristics of an Effective Children's Ministry

I want to suggest seven basic principles that can help churches see how children's ministry can fit into their strategy to truly impact the next generation.

1. Biblically-based lessons.
    A recent book by creationist Ken Ham and researcher Britt Beemer sent shock waves throughout evangelical circles by identifying their "Sunday school syndrome" as affecting scores of traditional churches. In *Already Gone: Why Your Kids Will Quit Church and What You Can Do to Stop It,* Ham and Beemer argue that "most Sunday school material just teaches stories! Most Sunday school teachers don't know how to answer the skeptical questions of the day. Sunday school is not preparing the children for what they will be taught at school; it is not preparing them to be able to defend the Christian faith."

    Their point, although perhaps somewhat overstated, is well taken. It's very important that we base our children's ministry lessons on the "whole counsel of God" (Acts 20:27) instead of just a series of unrelated Bible stories. Our children may know the accounts of Abraham and Isaac, Noah and the Arc, David and Goliath, and Daniel in the lions' den, but do they really understand God's *grand story* of creation, fall, and redemption? Truly effective children's ministries will be characterized by the complete and creative teaching of the life-changing Word of God.

2. <u>Involved parents.</u>
    As I have emphasized elsewhere in this book, the real key to lasting spiritual growth for our kids is the collaborative efforts of parents and the church working together for that very purpose.

    If you are a church leader or parent, or if you serve in your church's ministry with emerging generations, I suggest that at some point very soon you take a close evaluative look at *Think Orange: Imagine the Impact when Church and Family Collide* by Reggie Joiner,[77] the founder of "The reThink Group." This philosophy has challenged my thinking about the imperative and Biblical strategy of these two institutions working together for the common goal of helping our children grow up and go on for God. Here's how their strategy is described on their web site (http://whatisorange.org): "What if church leaders and parents synchronized their efforts to fuel wonder, discovery and passion in the next generation? By combining the critical influences of the light of the church (yellow) and the love of the family (red) the *Orange Strategy* shows a generation who God is more effectively than either could alone."[78]

    Your children's ministry must include an element where parents are actively involved in the process of the church's educational and training commitments for children. Certainly, I understand that there will be children that attend your church from dysfunctional and disinterested families. However, no one has more potential to influence a child than a parent. That's why it is crucial that parents be included in your children's ministry as much as possible.

3. <u>A big-picture philosophy of educational ministries.</u>
   Here's another important principle to consider as you think about children's ministry – and that is the need for an overarching philosophy of educational ministries in the church that includes all generations. It's dangerous for the children's ministry and youth ministry to be in their own orbit away from the over-all programming strategy of the church. Yet, this is what happens all too often in so many traditional churches: the children's workers do their own thing, the youth workers do something else, and the adult ministries do something entirely different. It's critically important for all of these ministries to be on the same page with the same objective and the same kind of approaches for reaching those objectives. Someone in your church should be able to give immediate answers to the following questions:

   ✓ What is your church's philosophy of educational ministries? (In other words, what are you trying to accomplish?)
   ✓ How does your children's ministry tie into the youth ministry?
   ✓ How does your youth ministry tie into the adult ministries of the church?
   ✓ Are there intentional transitions between those age-group ministries?
   ✓ How are other generations involved in your church's age-group ministries?

4. <u>Creative, age-relevant, life-related curriculum.</u>
   The concept of *curriculum* "has its roots in the Latin word for race-course, explaining the curriculum as the course of deeds and experiences through which children become adults."[79] When most people think

of the idea of curriculum, their minds conjure thoughts of going to a Christian bookstore and selecting some book or materials to teach for the next section of class. But, actually that's not it at all. The correct meaning of the term implies a "race course" – with a set beginning and ending point. I often remind children's workers and youth workers to think of it like this, "What do you want your students to know by the time they leave your program?" Basically the proper understanding of curriculum is more like a college or university where certain specific courses are a required part of your major in order for you to graduate with the prescribed degree. It's a listing of what is required and what is necessary. (I share more information on this subject in my chapter "Teaching On Purpose with a Purpose" in *Pushing the Limits: Unleashing the Potential of Student Ministry*.[80]) A curriculum is a total educational plan of what should be taught when and how throughout the entire programming (or discipleship process) of the church.

Children's ministry absolutely requires creativity, age-relevant learning, and life-application teaching methods. These characteristics must be combined with an overall educational plan of what students should know, do, and believe in. That's the real purpose of a curriculum.

5. Godly, faithful, creative, gifted leaders and workers.
   Of course, adult leaders and teachers are also imperative for an effective children's program in the church. My wife and I thank God for the scores of influential church workers who cared enough to make an impact on our children when they were going through

our churches' educational ministries as children and teenagers. All church leaders must make sure that each children's worker is totally committed to Christ and is faithfully and consistently living for Him. That's the place to start. After that it's also important to recruit a team of creative and gifted teachers and workers who will be faithful to this aspect of your ministry over the long haul. You should also look for adults in all age ranges and from various life stages that are willing to serve in the children's ministry, and for people who have the ability and aptitude to serve alongside of parents with the goal of seeing children grow up into maturity in Christ. Once your team of workers has been recruited and is in place, it will also be important to introduce a plan to train those adult workers how to work with children, how to use the teaching materials, and how to best develop close, yet disciplined relationships with children.

6. <u>A safe learning environment.</u>
This particular point is also absolutely essential in today's safety-conscious, mega-protective family culture. It is critically important for churches to place an utmost priority on the protection of children and youth. I implore you to do your homework and research this aspect of your ministries through your local and state authorities and consult your church's liability insurance agent. In this age of "helicopter parents"[81] or even "stealth-fighter parents"[82] (parents who are "even more protective, digitally keyed-in for constant surveillance, sharp eyes on the target, and ready to strike at a moment's notice to defend their children's interests"[83]), it is imperative for churches

to take the utmost care for the minors that are entrusted to their care.

The role of parents combined with an authentic, Christ-like self-sacrificial love for children demands that classroom protection be a major emphasis. Our ministries should shout, "We care for your kids."

Our church just went through a renewed push to develop and initiate a church-wide child protection policy that includes background checks for all adult workers and a firm check-in and check-out procedure for parents dropping off and picking up their children. We also went through the tedious process of revising our church constitution so that our official church documents require compliance to the policy of actively caring for minors. More information about child protection policies can be obtained from your church's insurance company.[84]

7. Exposure to other age groups.
    As expressly stated throughout this book, another vital aspect of effective ministry is a church-wide commitment to developing inter-generational connections. It's critically important to develop a church culture that intentionally cross-pollinates the generations. (As I stated in the last point, these relationships must be built through a process that carefully adheres to the church's established child protection policy.) I also highly recommend a team of adult children's workers that especially includes married couples. I am not saying that Godly and committed singles cannot or should not work with children. It's just that using married couples as children's workers provides a consistent model and

presents another layer of accountability for safety and protection.

Children's ministry can be a virtual launching pad for the development of natural inter-generational connections. If adults and teenagers alike are encouraged to actively participate in children's classes, programs, and activities (again with the proper background checks, etc.), they will naturally grow up accepting the concept of building growing relationships with Godly, significant adults.

There is one other matter that deserves some comment on this subject. I personally do not believe that it is wise for a church to utilize teenagers on a regular basis as teachers or workers in the children's department. We should remember that teenagers are adolescents and they do not have the maturity to handle some of the serious and intricate situations that may be associated with children and their parents. Plus, I hold the view that teenagers need to be actively engaged with their own peers (in youth group), and need to develop the habit of being an enthusiastic attendee and participant in their church's worship and preaching services. Undoubtedly, Godly teenagers can and should serve and utilize their gifts within a local church setting. Frankly, it's a shame that so many churches are taking teenagers away from home on missions trips to give them an opportunity to teach the Bible and to serve in various aspects of children's ministry instead of giving them occasions to do that in their home church. So, this too must be balanced – give spiritually vibrant young people opportunities to serve and teach children, but balance those avenues of ministry alongside of regular attendance and involvement in the church services.

I also advise churches to always include mature adults as teachers and leaders in working with children. This level of cooperation between older teachers and maturing teenagers within children's ministry can provide an invaluable level of hands-on training, priceless opportunities for mentoring, and the development of lasting inter-personal and inter-generational relationships.

A Biblically-sound, family-friendly, life-related, safe, philosophy-driven, inter-generational children's ministry must be one of the most dynamic and effective aspects of church life. Certainly, parents must be actively involved and must partner with the church in making the Gospel and the spiritual growth of younger generations a top priority – maybe better said, the top priority. However, we all must realize that children's ministry was never intended to be a terminal program. It must be an indispensable part of the overall structure and direction of the total church. Our objective, of course, is not for emerging generations to remain as children or spiritual babies. We must be passionate advocates for children's ministries that help our kids mature and go on for God (see Ephesians 4:13-14).

Chapter Seven: Youth Ministry
"That the Next Generation Would Know"

The statistics are indeed startling. Many, many young people are walking away from church after being active in church and youth group during their childhood and teen years. A report from *The Barna Group* may have brought this scenario to the attention of the general evangelical public a few years ago with this revealing title, *"Most Twentysomethings Put Christianity on the Shelf Following Spiritually Active Teen Years."*[85] The widespread reaction has been to blame youth ministry. The arguments are something like this: "the youth group is entertainment-based," "it separates generations," and "it replaces parents as the primary influencers over young people."[86] It's easy to blame the youth ministry. But, I wonder...

Of course, the root of this situation lies within the family. Parents are the primary influence over their children even as the kids age into their late teenage years. But, ecclesiastically-speaking, what if the problem actually rests on "big church"? Maybe today's students love and profit greatly from youth ministry; and because the church as a whole is nothing like the youth ministry, the kids hate it and therefore walk away looking for something else. Maybe youth ministry has it right. Let's not forget that most people accept Christ and many make lifetime spiritual decisions when they are young.[87] Teenagers go on more short-term missions trips than adults[88] – and more Christian teens share their faith than do Christian adults.[89] I have wondered for years why we don't manage our churches like youth groups. In fact, I have told youth ministry students somewhat factiously for years that if senior pastors would run their churches like youth pastors run their youth groups we would have more growing churches.

Please don't dismiss this premise without thinking it through. I am absolutely convinced that this problem is serious enough that we should carefully examine the phenomenon from all sides of the issue. We must not dismiss a God-honoring, Biblically-based, and culturally-relevant ministry like youth work due to a prejudicial hypothesis or because of an over-reaction to statistics. A careful and historical look at youth ministry will reveal some amazing results from what is now being called traditional youth ministry.[90]

I must admit, however, that I have seen significant weaknesses in some local church youth programs. I have identified some of those deficiencies below. But, before we unilaterally accept these flaws and come to the conclusion that traditional youth ministry is failing, we'll take a look at the kind of church youth ministry that is "working" and is producing Godly high school graduates who greatly desire to go on for Christ as adults.

Some Reasons Why Youth Ministry Might Fail

There may be certain common denominators within some churches that lead to the mass departure of young people following high school graduation. Here are some observations based upon my 35-plus years of active involvement in local church youth ministry. (I'll discuss this subject in greater detail in Chapter 12.)

Activity-based youth ministry

If the church's youth ministry is built upon programs and activities, your graduates will probably walk away after they graduate. Young adults can and will find their entertainment elsewhere. The appeal of amusement parks and concerts fades away fairly quick. In fact, many youth workers tell me that some of their high school juniors and seniors are actually dropping out of youth group early for the same reasons. Youth workers, please be careful of running the same activity schedule year after year, so that your seniors have the same basic schedule as ninth graders. Believe me – they'll get bored and frustrated with that kind of programming.

Program-based youth ministry

Another reason why high school graduates walk away from regular involvement in church is if the youth group has been characterized by the rigid structure of a "boxed" youth program. These canned approaches are, in fact, designed to be terminal programs, with a specific, publicized ending point. There tends to be one final step or one top award to earn. That's the point. The students finish the program and they're done. What else is there to do? In the program-based approach to youth ministry, it is very difficult to transfer the loyalty generated throughout the years of dedication to the program to the church as a whole. It's no wonder they walk away. I understand that many of the popular, para-church youth ministry programs came into existence with a passion to reach kids for Christ and a desire to be culturally relevant, and I applaud them for those motivations. I'm just talking here about some basic reasons why teenagers may choose to walk away from church following the completion of the program.

Personality-based youth ministry

A common indictment of many church youth ministries is the tendency to center the ministry around the strong personality of a charismatic and magnetic youth pastor or youth leader. Strong personalities may attract impressionable high school students, and it seems to make sense for churches to do that – until the inevitable transition between personalities. If the teenagers are attracted to and ministered to by the presence of one strong personality, it will be very difficult for them to transition into the ministries of the church as a whole without the involvement of that strong personality or other equally strong personalities.

Generationally-based youth ministry

As I have emphasized throughout this book, a church is making a mistake if it totally separates its youth from the overall life of the church. In the long run this hurts students because they do not develop significant relationships with a number of influential adults. I have spent a long time specializing in local church youth ministry and I am a strong proponent of peer ministry. Christian kids need friendships with other Christian kids. Plus, teenagers have always been better at reaching their peers than adult youth workers.[91] However, a balanced youth ministry must feature strong inter-generational connections alongside traditional peer-to-peer youth groups.

Narcissism-based youth ministry

Akin to the "activity-based" model of youth ministry is a narcissistic approach where churches seek to entertain teenagers by providing almost everything they want. If the kids want to go skiing, they go on ski trips. If the kids want to go swimming, they take them to the beach. This approach will ultimately produce self-absorbed and self-centered graduates who believe the church is all about them. When they are asked to transition into the church's adult ministries, they'll struggle to fit into a program that is not centered on entertainment and narcissism. The undeveloped youth mindset may respond positively to an entertainment-based approach, but adult maturity realizes there's more to life than getting everything you want.

We've all seen some youth programs like the ones I have described above. The tendency is to look at these flaws and come to the conclusion that all youth ministry isn't working. However, not all youth ministries are characterized by these particular weaknesses. Let's give youth ministry some credit. For instance, I personally know many, many youth pastors who are completely committed to a Biblically-based ministry, who are working hard to support parents of teenagers, and whose ministries are plugged-in to the overall philosophy of the church. Friends, it is imperative and essential to look at both sides of this issue before rushing to a quick, all too stereotypical indictment.

Some Positive Attributes of Youth Ministry that Maybe Should Be Adopted by the Church as a Whole

Speakers and writers love to quote the dropout statistics. We understand that the number one time for people to quit going to church is immediately following high school graduation. As I mentioned above, it's easy (maybe too easy) to blame youth ministry for the departure.[92] One writer puts it this way, "Almost everyone involved in youth ministry agrees that something is wrong. But how bad is it really? It is bad enough that it is stimulating a lot of interest in youth ministry circles and visible enough for major news outlets and research organizations to report on it." The author goes onto conclude that "the public collapse of modern youth ministry is reaching such legendary proportions that people involved in various functions of church life want to talk about how to repair it."[93] He continues, "The hunger for relevancy and attractiveness has driven youth ministry into various forms of hipster idolatry. This craving for something better and cooler than God has made youth ministry look more like a rock concert, coffee bar, or club than the holy people of God."[94]

It is easy to charge some of the youth ministry extremes (see my admittedly abridged list of common denominators above) for this mass exodus from church. However, this "state of emergency"[95] deserves a comprehensive examination of the big picture of church ministries instead of concentrating on just one side of the coin. I recently received a personal e-mail from a veteran youth pastor responding to the critics of youth ministry and youth pastors: I hate the stereotype that youth pastors are all about fun and games "and maybe a Bible-themed lesson." I know those guys exist and probably more than I wish. But, no credence is given to the youth pastors in the trenches who are working with families, who are working with the fatherless, who are working with the practical-orphans, who are pointing children to the Word of God and watching them grow up to serve Him all over the world. No credence is given to those who are working with parents, not against them; those who are uniting the generations not dividing them.[96]

I had an interesting conversation a few months ago with an experienced and knowledgeable youth pastor who serves in a balanced and respected church in the northern Midwest.[97] We engaged in a lengthy discussion about why this exodus from church is happening among college-age young adults who were once actively engaged in various church youth groups. We talked about the facets of traditional youth ministry that may lead to this scenario occurring so universally in various denominations and fellowships of churches. I began to rehearse some of the common characteristics of conventional youth groups that undoubtedly lead to a migration from church once the energy and enthusiasm of youth ministry had faded into the typical adult world of the church.

My friend then made a comment which has challenged my thinking ever since: "Perhaps we've got it all wrong," he mused. "What if it's the other way around? What if our kids leave the church because traditional adult ministries are irrelevant, boring, and impractical to them? We're blaming the youth group, but it might be the church as a whole that is the problem."

I am very seldom at a loss for words, but that afternoon the questions from this veteran youth worker stopped me in my tracks. What if he was right? Maybe, just maybe, we are doing things right in youth group. Maybe we're on to something there that the church as a whole should embrace and adopt. Maybe the characteristics of a typical youth ministry are exactly the things that would keep students in church. The common reaction to this exit from church is to blame the youth ministry and to assume that the adult world in our churches is organized and structured correctly.

We hear the statistics and tend to blame student ministry for its weaknesses. We cite our failure to develop healthy and growing inter-generational relationships and the lack of clear Biblical teaching as the reasons our kids walk away from church. I've often wondered why our churches tend to develop one style of ministry philosophy for students and a totally different ministry approach for adults. What if the church as a whole would adopt a *youth group approach* to ministry? Maybe the answer to this question is more important than we could ever imagine.

Here's another imperative question to think through. What if churches would implement a holistic and comprehensive ministry strategy that would seamlessly transition children into youth ministry and then teenagers into adult ministry?

My friend's question drove me to begin a process of outlining the basic ingredients of a successful, effective, and Biblically-based youth ministry. I will add flesh to these characteristics in future writing projects, but I will identify some incredibly positive elements of youth ministry here in an effort to help readers crystallize their thinking on this scenario.

Some positive characteristics of youth ministry (not listed in any priority order)

There are several things that church youth ministry is doing right. As I mentioned above, it is my conviction that the church as a whole should proactively and intentionally incorporate these 13 strategic characteristics into its basic fabric and framework.

1. A ministry based on a Biblical and practical philosophy (2 Timothy 3:10-17).

Most youth pastors understand that their ministries must be built upon a sound and logical philosophy of ministry that is both practical (in other words – it works) and Biblical. The essential nature of a philosophy-based ministry has been ingrained into the youth ministry culture from long-time youth ministry gurus such as Jack Wyrtzen (the founder of Word of Life[98]), Frank Hamrick (the founder of Positive Action for Christ[99]), and Dann Spader (the founder of SonLife[100]), and it has permeated youth ministry education at the Christian college and seminary level since the earliest days of this academic discipline.[101]

Other areas of church ministry understand the importance of developing a set philosophy of ministry; but undoubtedly, youth ministry has led the way in championing this principle as a foundational imperative. Trained and experienced youth pastors understand that a Biblical and practical philosophy of ministry must include a clear and concise mission statement and realistic, specific, and all-inclusive means to accomplish that objective in the lives of teenagers. These professional pastors are discerning enough to recognize that their ministries are terminal in nature – with set beginning and ending points. Youth ministry in most churches here in the United States deals with *teenagers* – adolescents from around 13 to 18 years of age. These educated and qualified specialists understand that their ministries are just one part of a larger scope of total church ministry. Youth ministry is not an end in itself, but is a key ingredient of developing fully-devoted, mature followers of Christ who should go on living for Christ long after their days as high school students. Biblical youth ministry must be intentional and must include a big-picture approach.

I base my own personal philosophy of youth ministry on the Apostle Paul's instructions to his student Timothy in 2 Timothy 3:10-17. Here Paul prompts his disciple to remember the influences upon his life that led to his spiritual maturity: the systematic teaching of Scripture, the modeling of spiritual maturity, everyday application of Biblical principles, and a consistent parental influence. (A fuller explanation of my philosophy of youth ministry is found in the Appendix.)

2. A ministry built around a complete Biblical educational strategy (Ephesians 4:11-16).

   Youth ministry, along with children's ministry, came into existence with a clear educational emphasis. The cultural attitude was that youth learned differently (than children or adults) and had different educational needs. Even to this day youth workers understand the developmental nature of an effective ministry to youth and therefore make educational ministries (e.g., Sunday school and youth group meetings) the usual focus of their programming efforts. In many churches, the church educational system is built around a "scope and sequence," or what is often called "curriculum." Many church leaders will recall the poster-sized charts from Sunday school curriculum publishers (e.g., Scripture Press, David C. Cook, Accent Publications, and denominational Sunday school publishers) showing what topics the company's material would cover for each age group throughout the entire church.

The point was for youth workers to have a complete educational plan for what the students would study all throughout their years in high school. Youth ministry being, as already described, a terminal program, has a specific starting point and ending point. Students enter the youth ministry as early junior highers (or sometimes called middle schoolers) and leave the youth ministry as high school graduates. Most youth workers I know understand this concept and have a detailed plan of what they want to accomplish and what the students should learn during their years in the church's teen ministry. Adolescence is a learning and maturing experience. Youth workers recognize that they, along with the students' parents, have a responsibility to clearly, creatively, and completely communicate Biblical truth in a way that relates to the lives of teenagers. They have a passion to teach the "whole counsel of God" (Acts 20:27 KJV) and they want the students to know what the Bible says and how It applies to their lives.

I am convinced that other church ministries should be as passionate about a total educational plan or "scope and sequence" as youth workers are. Other church leaders must also institute a complete educational plan that focuses on *"everything I have commanded you"* (Matthew 28:20) and *"All Scripture"* (2 Timothy 3:16).

(For a more thorough treatment of the use of "curriculum" in church ministry, readers can consult *Teaching on Purpose with a Purpose*, my chapter in a book I co-edited, along with my good friend, Mike Calhoun, *Pushing the Limits: Unleashing the Potential of*

Student Ministry, published by Thomas Nelson, 2006.[102])

3. <u>A ministry that builds habits of basic spiritual disciplines (James 1:22).</u>
    In my travels over the past several years I have visited churches of all sizes who would tout their commitment to children's ministry because they use Awana,[103] or some other similar packaged program. These same churches would emphasize the main priorities of those programs as a way for children to learn the Bible, and as an evangelistic outreach into the community. They see the importance of children memorizing Scripture, and yet older age groups in the church don't do it. I have also found it somewhat hypocritical for church youth ministries to emphasize the importance of young people having daily devotions, or daily *Quiet Time,*[104] and yet that spiritual discipline is rarely stressed for adults. Programs for younger ages seem to stress habits of basic spiritual disciplines that are not highlighted throughout the whole church. It's time to recognize that children's ministry and youth ministry got this aspect of their ministries right, and implement a regime of spiritual disciplines in the life of the entire church.

4. <u>A ministry that equips parents to be the primary spiritual influence in their children's lives (Ephesians 6:1-4).</u>
    Youth workers often get a "bad rap" for trying to supplant parental influence over the lives of teenagers. Author Steve Wright, in *reThink: Decide for Yourself is Student Ministry Working,* makes this statement about this issue, "The harsh reality is…when youth pastors are handed all the spiritual responsibility,

teens graduate from God when they graduate from student ministry."[105] Actually, I have found the opposite of this to be true in scores of churches I have visited over the past three-plus decades. Most youth pastors and youth workers I know work very hard to encourage and equip parents. They crave parental involvement in the church youth ministry and desperately want to work alongside parents in a collaborative effort to help maturing teenagers go on for God. These caring and dedicated specialists are doing everything they can to support parents and are faithfully seeking to communicate with them about the details and functions of the youth ministry. As youth ministry has "come of age" in this discipline's professionalization[106] over the years, the typical scenario of a young 20-something youth pastor who is more concerned with fun-and-games than he is with equipping and Biblical teaching is probably long gone. Many, many churches have replaced the entertainment-driven, parental-isolated model with a philosophy of ministry that definitely includes a major commitment to a formula of partnering with parents[107] for the development of lifelong faith[108] in young people. The collaborative efforts of church youth workers working alongside parents in the spiritual development of young people are powerful. This idea can be an effective blueprint for all areas of church programming – and it is truly a pattern for authentic inter-generational ministry. (Much more is said about the church partnering with parents in Chapters 4 and 14.)

5. A ministry that calls young people to make a lifetime commitment to Christ (Romans 10:9-10).

One of the hallmarks of evangelical youth ministry has been the call for teenagers to make public decisions for Christ. The technique of giving "invitations" for those responding to "come forward" for counseling and to make a public commitment was widely popularized in the early ministry of youth evangelists such as Billy Graham, Torrey Johnson, Percy Crawford, and Jack Wyrtzen - among others (see earlier references in this book to the history of youth ministry). I've never seen certifiable statistics that would confirm the validity of this statement, but I've heard for years and years about the great number of life-changing commitments that were made for Christ during people's teenage years as a result of youth groups and youth ministry events. Some anecdotal evidence may substantiate this claim. I spent many years of my ministry life as a speaker in a wide variety of youth and youth ministry events. These experiences have led me to believe that young people are very, very receptive to God's call and they are seemingly very willing to genuinely and publically respond to what God is leading them to do. I understand the objections to "alter-calls" and the corresponding *easy-believe-ism* that is often attributed to popular evangelical youth events. However, the actual, God-ordained, life-changing decisions made for Christ during so many people's teenage years give credence to the importance of this aspect of youth ministry. I believe in the call for genuine and public life commitments so much that I have wondered for years why we don't do this as often in adult ministries as well. We must never forget that God uses His Word to change people's lives (Romans 10:17). We must emphasize the clear and complete presentation of the Gospel of Jesus Christ in all of our church ministries to all age groups.

6. <u>A ministry that includes specific opportunities for Biblical and culturally-sensitive worship (John 4:21-24).</u>

Few can ignore the synergistic relationship between youth ministry and music. From its earliest days as an organized discipline, youth ministry has intentionally utilized the influence of music as an integral part of its strategy to minister to teenagers. Early proponents of this idea of incorporating music in youth ministry were people like Percy Crawford, Jack Wyrtzen, Torrey Johnson, and Jim Rayburn.[109] Rayburn was the founder of Young Life and the author of the oft-quoted statement, "It's a sin to bore a kid with the Gospel."[110] One youth ministry historian lists three characteristics of these early youth rallies: "a large auditorium, enthusiastic music, and preaching appealing to young people."[111] The trend to feature music in youth ministry continued with the *Jesus People* events of the late 1960s and early 1970s and continues to recent years with events such as *Jesus Camp*, *Teen Mania*, and the seemingly ubiquitous Christian-rock festivals.[112]

As a non-musician, I will admit that I believe the current emphasis on music in youth ministry may have become out of balance. Far too many youth events have taken the use of music to an extreme. I have been a speaker at many youth events where it seems that the time taken for music is at an inordinate level as compared to the time given to the speaker. But, youth ministry is to be credited for its long tradition of offering teenagers God-honoring, yet culturally-relevant music as an expression of worship toward the Lord. Maybe all of us should admit that the church has been historically very slow at changing its musical expressions as the musical tastes of emerging generations changed. Youth ministry has taken a great deal of heat and criticism from older generations for emphasizing *contemporary* music, and yet each previous generation also went through a metamorphosis of music tastes.[113] The church as a whole would do well to learn the positive and practical lessons that youth ministry has taught us about the importance of utilizing Biblical and culturally-sensitive music for worship.

7. <u>A ministry where participants regularly have focused time away from the daily routines of life (Mark 6:31-32).</u>
    The Christian camping industry has played a profound role in evangelical youth ministry. Historically and practically, youth ministry has featured the importance of getting participants away from the stress and hassles of everyday life and into the peaceful serenity of God's nature for extended time away from the daily routines of life.[114] Youth workers of all kinds have valued Christian camping as an integral part of their programming efforts. Churches take kids to camp and host various retreats with the motive of seeing God do something specific in their hearts and lives. It amazes me to think that churches see the importance of camping for children and teenagers and yet often do not emphasize it for adults.

8. <u>A ministry that provides opportunities for believers to experience life-related fellowship with others from their own peer group (1 John 3:16-17).</u>

Youth ministry came into existence for two basic purposes: to teach the Bible to teenagers, and to provide opportunities for Christian young people to fellowship with other Christian young people. The early youth events, like Jack Wyrtzen's "Word of Life Rallies" in New York City and Torrey Johnson's "Victory Rallies" in Chicago,[115] were developed and organized around those two basic ideals. The focus, of course, was to present the Gospel to youth, but the glue that connected the thousands of young people to each other was the opportunity for Christian fellowship. The emergence of an American youth culture meant that teenagers and young adults needed to converge with peers around the commonality of a central, core belief – the Gospel message of salvation through Jesus Christ. This unity meant that these young people had something very much in common, they had *fellowship*; and this peer connection became something very unique and very special about youth ministry. Church youth ministry has always been characterized by the opportunity for fellowship among Christian young people. This fellowship is so special, so exceptional, that the church as a whole should adopt the youth ministry practice of providing regular and creative opportunities for it. God's people need to gather together around the true cohesiveness of their personal relationship with Christ and the doctrinal truth of Scripture. Believers need to experience genuine, life-related fellowship with other believers – and youth ministry has set the example for this practice.

9. <u>A ministry that includes hands-on training and experience in specific evangelistic outreach (Matthew 28:19-20 and Acts 1:8).</u>

Another incredibly positive characteristic of youth ministry has been its commitment to train teenagers how to share their faith.[116] Most youth workers understand the need to equip students in practical aspects of evangelism and have developed a four-tiered emphasis on outreach into their ministries (life-style evangelism, public school outreach, "visitation" or organized group evangelism, and evangelistic events).[117] Youth workers should also get credit for popularizing short-term missions trip as a way for teenagers to get hands-on training and experience in cross-cultural evangelism. According to a recent *Christianity Today* article, over 2 million American high school students participate in short-term missions trips each year. Plus, more money is now being spent on short-term trips than is given annually for career missions.[118] Youth missions trips have grown into a cultural phenomenon and a full-blown industry.[119] My point here is that youth ministry should receive some recognition and acknowledgement for setting the pace for other age groups in the church regarding evangelism. I have had personal experience with several church youth pastors and volunteer youth workers alike that are purposefully and carefully developing an Acts 1:8 strategy of implementing the concentric circles of outreach ("*Jerusalem, Judea, Samaria, and the ends of the earth*") into their youth ministries. Oh, that churches as a whole would be that intentional about their evangelistic outreach!

10. <u>A ministry that provides appropriate means of service and ministry (Ephesians 4:11-16).</u>
    A desire to get teenagers plugged into ministry has also been a trademark of evangelical youth ministry. The early days of youth ministry were characterized

and influenced by youth-led programming led by organizations such as Christian Endeavor,[120] which traces its history back to the late 1800s. I grew up as a church kid and was active in various avenues of youth ministry in the late 1960s and early 1970s. I clearly remember my home church's "youth night services" where the teenagers led some of the church's evening services. It was during one of these meetings my senior year that I first preached a sermon in public. I vividly remember being asked to speak for 20 minutes. However, due to my fear and nervousness, I quit in four minutes after going through my notes and talking as fast as I possibly could.

Today, many youth workers are making service and ministry a key component of their ministries. As I already mentioned, short-term missions trips are one way this is happening *en masse*. Through the avenue of these trips, teenagers are given multiple opportunities to serve and share their faith. The ideal focus of ministry, however, must be the local church. Providing or creating ways for teenagers to serve the Lord in and through the church has been a distinguishing attribute of many youth ministries. I can make this statement with confidence after visiting several churches without a significant, organized youth ministry where the teenagers' only option for ministry was to wait until the older generations passed from the scene. It's important to remember that God's plan for the church is that every believer should be actively serving Him (Ephesians 4:11-16 and 1 Corinthians 12:12-31). The commitment many youth workers make to involve as many teens as possible in ministry is something the entire church should replicate.

11. A ministry that offers true Biblical accountability (Hebrews 10:24).

"Community" is an oft-used buzzword[121] in Christian circles today describing a unified body life that ideally is to be present in individual local churches. The basic concept is that Christ intended spiritual formation or growth only to happen in and through involvement in His church. It was never His intent for believers to live for Him in an individualized vacuum without a local assembly of the Body of Christ to assist in the process of spiritual growth. Youth ministry leads the way on this one, too. Youth pastors have figured out how to instill accountability and positive peer pressure in their youth groups. When our children were teenagers they never wanted us to go away so that they had to miss youth group – they loved it that much. Their friends were there, they loved the adult youth workers, they actively participated in the times of worship and Bible study, and they took every opportunity they could to invite their unsaved, unchurched friends to the meetings. Youth group was that important to them.

I've often wondered why church life isn't like that for adults. Even a cursory reading of Acts and the Epistles seems to reveal a unity in the early church that is very seldom present in churches today. The church was the center of life and faith for the early believers and it was their top priority. The church provided a format for spiritual growth and there was a very real sense of genuine accountability in the church community (2 Corinthians 2:5-11 and Philippians 4:10-19).

12. <u>A ministry that presents life-related discipling led by
    Godly and mature leaders (2 Timothy 2:2).</u>

    Another key attribute of youth ministry is the focus
    on real-life discipleship. I understand that there are
    some who disdain the idea of true discipleship with
    youth. One of them was the late Mike Yaconelli, the
    co-founder of Youth Specialties. In his article "Hur-
    ried Discipleship," he wrote, "Youth-oriented disci-
    pleship programs have reduced disciples to cheer-
    leaders and political organizers. Discipleship has
    been turned into a measurable, external activity in-
    stead of an immeasurable, internal lack of activity.
    Spending time evangelizing has replaced spending
    time with Jesus, and sharing our faith with others has
    replaced growing in our faith with Jesus." But Ya-
    conelli adds, "there is another, more serious problem.
    Young people are…well…young, which means they
    are immature, confused by their hormones, inexperi-
    enced, naïve and idealistic. None of these qualities
    are bad, in fact, they are wonderful gifts of youth that
    are needed in the church, but they are not neutral.
    Simply put, discipleship is a lifelong process, not a
    youth activity."[122]

    However, almost every youth worker understands
    the importance of discipling the next generation.
    Youth pastors and volunteer youth workers alike cite
    the familiar Biblical instruction in 2 Timothy 2:2 as a
    mantra of their philosophy of youth ministry: *"And
    the things you have heard me say in the presence of many
    witnesses entrust to reliable people who will also be quali-
    fied to teach others."* The Biblical pattern of one genera-
    tion spiritually reproducing itself in the lives of the
    next generation has been imbedded into the frame-
    work of youth ministry, and many youth workers are

doing all they can to make disciples (Matthew 28:19-20). They understand the time commitment it takes to truly disciple someone and are willing to build the amount of time it takes into their ministries.[123] Sure, there are many churches out there that understand the importance of true discipleship. Yet, I can say with all confidence that the commitment to discipleship has been more readily visible in youth ministry than it has in other age groups in the church. Let's learn from youth ministry and intentionally incorporate discipling the next generation into the overall scope of church life and function.

13. <u>A ministry that provides healthy and growing inter-generational connections (1 Thessalonians 2:8).</u>
     There's one final characteristic that merits inclusion in our conversation of the positive features of youth ministry, and that is the development of significant inter-generational relationships. As I explained in Chapter 5, evangelical churches have traditionally been one-generational or multi-generational, segregating generations for training, fellowship, and in many situations, for worship and Bible study. In contrast, youth ministry has historically been inter-generational. I realize this statement may seem contradictory with other parts of this book, so let me explain. Almost every youth group I have ever seen has understood the importance of having a team of adult youth workers ministering to a group of teenagers. The only exceptions to that observation were smaller churches with very few teenagers and a corresponding small group of adults. Even then, the very nature of youth ministry is characterized by the positive relationship that caring, Godly adults can have with teenagers. Of course, other age-segregated ministries

(e.g., Sunday school, Vacation Bible School, Children's Church) utilize committed adults to minister to children and adolescents. But, youth ministry has long been differentiated by select adults building relationships with teenagers.[124] Again, I've wondered for years why the church collectively does not adopt this inter-generational, relationship-building strategy. It makes sense, and this very basic plan (older people building interpersonal relationships with younger people) is a prime example of mentoring.[125] (See Chapter 11 for a broader description of building an inter-generational, church-based mentoring ministry.) An intentional plan for connecting the generations by asking older adults to mentor younger people finds its root in youth ministry and can be put into practice in any church.

The statistics *are* startling, and it's easy to blame youth ministry and in some cases it can be blamed. But, as we have seen, there may be more to this issue. There are many Biblical and practical characteristics of youth ministry that should be instituted into the church as a whole. Perhaps if the church functioned more like youth ministry then young adults would want to stay engaged in the church following high school. We'll take a look at that age group more in the next chapter.

Chapter Eight: Young Adult and College-Age Ministry
"Don't Let Anyone Look Down on You Because You Are Young"

A generation is missing from the church in America. Young adults aren't there. Here's the crisis in a nutshell, "More than two-thirds of young churchgoing adults in America drop out of church between the ages of eighteen and twenty-two!"[126] Over the past several years I have talked to dozens of pastors and other church leaders who admitted that their church's ministry to college-age young adults is the weakest aspect of their ministries. As one author observes, "The church is losing the generational battle...Multitudes are dropping out of church."[127] I've visited numerous churches that have a very active youth ministry and who are strategically ministering to middle-age and older adults, but where a relevant and significant ministry to young adults is conspicuously absent.

David Kinnaman, the president of the Barna Group research organization puts it this way in his new book, *You Lost Me: Why Young Christians Are Leaving Church... And Rethinking Faith*: "The ages eighteen to twenty-nine are the black hole of church attendance; this age segment is 'missing in action' from most congregations." Kinnaman goes on to add, "overall, there is a 43 percent drop-off between the teen and early adult years in terms of church engagement. These numbers represent about eight million twentysomethings who were active churchgoers as teenagers but who will no longer be particularly engaged in a church by their thirtieth birthday."[128]

According to recent United States Department of Labor statistics, over 70% of recent high school graduates attend college, which sets an all-time record.[129] Dubbed the *Millennials* by well-known generational researchers Neil Howe and William Strauss, this demographic cohort is now entering the world of young adulthood: "America has well over ninety million Millennials. By the time future immigrants join their U.S.-born peers, this generation will probably top one hundred million members, making it nearly a third bigger than the Boomers... Millennials will greatly exceed Gen Xers, edge out Boomers, and tower over every earlier generation in America."[130]

It's somewhat discouraging to think that more Americans than ever before are members of this age group and yet the church is doing so little about it. But perhaps that trend is about to change. I have always noticed that ministry movements tend to follow population growth. Youth ministry came into vogue because of the growing number of teenagers (see Chapter 2) and church planting efforts that came to fruition believing that aging Baby Boomers would someday return to church as *seekers.*[131] Now the population bubble features Millennials – the largest generation in U.S. history, most of whom are young adults. It's about time for the church to respond with salient and relevant ministries for this burgeoning generation.

Where to Begin?

I live in a college town. I recently met a young girl who is attending college here so I asked her if anyone from her home church recommended a good church to her while she completes her studies. To my amazement she replied that no one from her home church, including her parents or pastors, had said anything to her about finding a good church in the town where she is attending college. Of course, I suggested that she should try our church, but that conversation left me wondering.

Are pastors and youth pastors talking to their church's graduating high school seniors about getting plugged in to a good church while they are away from home attending college? According to a report from the Barna Research Group, "only

38% of youth pastors and 36% of senior pastors say they frequently discuss college plans with their students."[132]

That's amazing to me. The majority of pastors and youth pastors never talk to their high school graduates about what they are going to do after high school. Our kids are leaving the church after they graduate from high school and we are simply letting them walk away?

Pastors and church leaders, I wholeheartedly believe that there are proactive and simple things you can do to help your church's graduating seniors transition out of youth group and into the life God has for them as emerging adults. I ask you to prayerfully consider these suggestions and then take the action steps necessary to implement some of the following ideas into the fabric of your church.

1. Schedule individual appointments with your church's graduating seniors to talk about God's will for their lives.

   High school graduation is a tangible rite of passage in today's society. It's a big deal. Your high school graduates are transitioning from the cocoon world of their parents' home and the church youth group into the looming and scary world of adulthood. So, be intentional about this fantastic opportunity and schedule personal appointments with each graduating senior in your church. Believe me, most of them are looking for some help on how to determine God's will for their lives and they would greatly appreciate a gentle, yet probing talk from their pastor about that. Of course, many of your graduates have already made plans for their futures. Some are entering the workforce, others are going to college, and some may be enlisting in the military. This is the perfect occasion to meet with each one of these members of your flock to talk with them about God's plan and direction for their lives. (Don't forget that this might also be the ideal time to give each senior a gift from the church honoring them for their high school graduation.)

2. <u>Talk to the students' parents to see if you can help them.</u>
    High school graduation is also the perfect opportunity to talk to the kids' parents about the future. This is probably a time of high tension for them as well. They have fretted for years about the money for college or about what the world will be like for their children. A brief heart-to-heart pep talk from their pastor or their kids' youth pastor would be much appreciated. You can discuss how to help the grads stay connected to the church following graduation. You can also help the parents find a good, solid, Bible-believing church for their graduate in the city where they'll be living next year. This talk would be a great encouragement to them.

3. <u>Identify those you believe are called to full-time vocational ministry.</u>
    God is still in the business of calling young people to serve Him. Some of them may be leaving your church youth group this year. Have you talked to them about vocational ministry? You could take this opportunity to talk to these individuals about the honors and privileges of serving the Lord full time. You might be able to offer them some practical advice on attending a Bible college or on what they can do now to prepare for full-time ministry later. If you have sensed that the hand of God is on certain individual students in your youth group, why don't you talk to them about it? Now is the perfect time.

4. <u>Develop a team of adults to keep in touch with the graduates while they are away from home.</u>

Here's another simple, but proactive idea for your church to consider. Why not build a team of adults in your church who will continue to communicate with your high school graduates after they leave your church? This team could consist of parents, grand-parents, and other interested adults. You may want to also consider adding younger high school students to this team as well. Encourage them to team up to secure the grads' mailing addresses and phone num-bers while they are away and to outline a specific plan to send them regular updates from the church, and perhaps even "care packages" while they are away from home. Of course, it is very important that your graduates know that their home church is pray-ing specifically for them while they are in college or in the military. So, ask the team to keep the list of your church's college students and members of the military in a conspicuous place on your church's regular prayer list.

5. <u>Recruit Godly, influential adults to welcome the high school graduates into the adult ministries of your church.</u>

This may be the most important idea of all. In most situations, your church's high school graduates would be no longer welcome in youth group. In our culture we tend to ask these new young adults to leave the youth ministry. Have you ever thought this through? Does your church have an intentional wel-coming committee that is committed to making your church's high school graduates feel wanted and wel-come in the adult ministries? As I mentioned before, it has been my experience that college-age ministries are some of the weakest areas in our churches. This may be the time to change that. Your new young adults don't want to be treated like teenagers any more. They want and need growing, healthy inter-generational relationships with other significant adults. Pastors and church leaders, let me remind you that this won't happen unless you put together a specific plan, and it starts with the active recruitment of specific Godly adults who are committed to mak-ing this emerging generation feel welcome in your church.

Developing a Ministry to College-Age Young Adults

I am convinced that any church can and should minister to the young adults by developing a few proactive and simple strategies. However, before I list those ideas, I must emphasize the fact that a ministry to this age group requires a commitment to do it. Many churches see high school kids leave the church following high school without tracking them to see where they are going to church or if they are even going on for God. We must close this gap and reinvest in this "missing generation" in our church. A ministry to this strategic age group begins with an investment of people resources. In other words, churches must decide to make college-age young adult ministry a top priority.

Here are some ideas on how your church can minister to this large and needy people group. You will notice right away that these ideas are ways to involve the whole church in a ministry to this age group. By implementing these simple ideas the church will truly build inter-generational relationships and connections.

1. Start by developing an opportunity to teach them God's Word.
   This really is a simple place to start. Does your church have a Sunday school class for college-age

young adults? If not, why not start one right away? Even your recent high school graduates need a place to study God's Word following their involvement in the youth group. Recruit significant, Godly adults in your church to lead this new ministry – and remember that this current generation is not looking for a revision of what they got in youth ministry. College-age students want to be treated as adults; it doesn't make sense for the church to give "fluff" to this age group when they are craving serious and important truth! If your church does not have the resources for a traditional Sunday School class, you could develop a regular time of Bible study for them instead. This age group needs Biblical answers that counter the various secular world views they are hearing in college. So, a teaching ministry is the place to start!

It's also important to note that this generation responds very positively to the clear, relevant, creative, and life-related presentation of Scripture. In other words, young adults want and need good preaching. As one author puts it, "We need to rediscover the Bible's grand narrative and teach an all-encompassing, multi-dimensional gospel. By showing how the life and death of Christ brings reconciliation with God, neighbor, creation, and self, young adults will hear the call to live as a prophetic sign of God's coming kingdom."[133]

2. <u>Provide Godly older mentors to build growing, personal relationships with this age group.</u>
   This age group needs older people! The church can and should provide Godly older mentors for this generation of emerging young adults. So many college-age para-church organizations tend to sepa-

rate young adults from the church by gathering groups of peers together on college or university campuses. Friends, this is a mistake. This age group desperately needs the church. The church can provide the human resources of a "family" of older adults who are willing to develop growing relationships and connections with college-age young adults. Encourage and teach your church's older adults to take the time to build personal relationships with younger adults.

3. <u>Supply opportunities for this age group to have fellowship.</u>

   Friends are the lifeline for this age group. That's another reason why churches should "do something" for young adults. The church can and should provide real fellowship with other members of this age group and with other ages. It's a shame, in some ways, that college and university students tend to develop their close friendships outside of the church. This generation is not looking for a series of "youth group games" or activities. A ministry to college-age young adults should look differently than that. Fellowship for this age group will probably feature hanging out around a cup of coffee instead of taking the members to the nearest amusement park.

4. <u>Give them leadership opportunities in the group and in your church as a whole.</u>

   One of the most effective ways to offer something to this age group is to give them some specific leadership responsibilities within the group and within the greater structure of the entire church. In other words, give them something to do. This generation can lead Bible studies and influence their peers. They are no longer teenagers – they are emerging adults. Give them leadership opportunities and work to train them for future positions of leadership in the church.

5. <u>Offer resources to help this age group become involved.</u>
   A very effective way to minister to this age group is for the church to supply resources for this generation that is in so much transition. Mentoring is one way to do that, but there is a variety of other ways that a church could minister to college-agers. One church I visited recently (located near a major university) hosts a meal for college students every Sunday afternoon. Another church provides transportation to and from the nearby college campuses. My home church recruited a team of families to host college-age students in their homes on Sunday afternoons. The point is that every local church has a supply of resources that could be utilized to minister to this age group. Ideas abound.

These simple ideas do not do justice to this important aspect of church programming. However, it is a shame for churches to do nothing – especially when the number one time people walk away from church is following high school. It's time to do something!

Ministering to Your Church's Young Adults While They are Away in School

Here are five practical suggestions for ministering to your church's college students who are away from your church while they are in college.

1. Encourage your church's college students to find a good church immediately when they arrive on campus.

    If nothing else, take the time to talk to the college students from your church who are away from home about finding a good, Bible-preaching church in the town they are attending school. You might also want to take the time to investigate the churches in the area where your students are living to make informed recommendations to them. This will not take a long time with the wealth of information available on the Internet. Make sure your young adults are plugged in to a good church nearby the college or university they are attending. Believe me – this is also important if your students are attending a Christian college or even a Bible college. Experts on this age group are saying that college-age habits are usually formed within the first two weeks they are away from home;[134] so this suggestion is very, very important for their spiritual growth and development while they are away in college.

2. Stay in touch with your church's college students in order to encourage them in their walk with God.

    Make sure you know their mailing address, e-mail address, and cell phone number so that you can stay in touch with them while they are away in college. Put it on your personal schedule to send them an e-mail or a text message just to find out how they are doing in college and to let them know that people from their home church are praying regularly for them. You can also use those means of communication to encourage them to get plugged in to a church near their campus.

3. <u>Send them a "love gift" from home within two weeks of when they arrive on campus.</u>

   Make sure your church sends them a care package (home-made chocolate chip cookies are a must for college students!) within a couple of weeks. You might also want to send them a gift card for a free pizza. Why don't you recruit a team of church people to handle this important detail? There's nothing like the encouragement from receiving a love gift from people back at home.

4. <u>Suggest ways they can stay connected with their home church while they are away at college.</u>

   College students often feel out of touch while they are away from their home church. Perhaps it would be a good idea to send each of them your church's weekly church bulletin and prayer request list. Put this simple practice on a tickler file as a reminder to send them this information on a regular basis.

5. <u>Recruit a team of people in your church to pray specifically for those students while they are in college.</u>

   I can't tell you how important it is for today's college students to know that caring people back home are praying regularly for them while they are away at school. Put together a complete list of all the young adults from your church who are away at college (and in the military, for that matter) and add them to your church's prayer list. Then make sure you re-mind your church people to pray for them regularly and faithfully. This simple act of prayer will be a real source of encouragement to your church's students who are studying away from home.

Please don't forget that these students are still your church's young people. Your church has invested so much in their lives during their formative years as children and youth. Don't drop the ball while they are away in college!

Cultural Shifts Facing Today's Young Adults

We've discussed some basic ways churches can minister to this age group, but before we conclude our conversation about college-age young adults we should talk about them as individuals. This generation has faced a series of cultural shifts that have had a considerable influence on their lives. These shifts have changed the landscape of an entire generation and it is important for the church to understand them.

1. <u>The changing role of higher education.</u>
   Enrollment in American colleges and universities has grown significantly over the past several years. In just a ten-year span, college attendance has grown by about 26%.[135] According to the Pew Research Center, about 40% of all young adults, ages 18 to 24, are currently enrolled in college.[136] This enrollment growth has been especially fueled by a sharp rise in students attending two-year community colleges that are currently boasting record enrollment rates.[137] Here's another interesting trend that merits our consideration: people taking college-level or above classes online is also drastically changing higher education. For several decades, the largest enrollment in traditional universities hovered around 70,000 students at both Ohio State University and Arizona State University. But by 2009, the internet-based school the University of Phoenix recorded a staggering 380,000 students.[138]

   I definitely understand that these statistics are likely to change and become invalid very quickly, but my point is this: this generation of young adults has lived through some very dramatic changes in higher education. The ramifications for church ministry are noteworthy. There are a lot of college-age students out there and churches must reach out to them. It's also important to note that more and more of your church's college-age young adults will not be leaving home to go to school.[139] These facts present great ministry opportunities for the church, including perhaps a lengthening of the amount of time a church can minister to them before they move on and leave home.

2. The lengthening of adolescence.

College ministry specialist Chuck Bomar points out that, for some, "College means four more years of putting off 'adult' decisions about work and family."[140] And in a recent *New York Times* article, Robin Marantz Henig adds that young adults are "forestalling the beginning of adult life."[141] Henig goes onto to expound on this new life stage:

> We're in the thick of what one sociologist calls 'the changing timetable for adulthood.' Sociologists traditionally define the 'transition to adulthood' as marked by five milestones: completing school, leaving home, becoming financially independent, marrying and having a child. In 1960, 77 percent of women and 65 percent of men had, by the time they reached 30, passed all five milestones. Among 30-year-olds in 2000, according to data from the United States Census Bureau, fewer than half of the women and one-third of the men had done so.[142]

105

Culture seems to have already identified the new phenomenon of lengthening adolescence and has labeled it "emerging adulthood."[143] Now some churches are beginning to recognize the importance of ministering to people in this particular stage of life. For instance, I recently noticed that one mega-church in the Midwest changed the title of their "high school pastor" to "high school and post-high school pastor." Their thought was to continue building "a continued relationship with a community that has already journeyed with them during their high school years."[144] Bomar also describes churches that have made efforts to minister to college-age people: "They've seen the detachment that comes after high school graduation and have worked hard to develop programs and services to help those college-age people stay connected to the church. Perhaps the most popular solution has been the 'contemporary service' model that…is intended to appeal to the late-adolescent and young adult age group."[145] The weaknesses of this approach seem to be obvious. Culture may be lengthening adolescence and may be postponing adult decisions, but if churches respond by extending age-segregation (separating youth and young adults from adults) even longer, the transition into adulthood is even harder and it can create even more division in the church. Conversely, churches must seek to develop growing inter-generational connections that will help these emerging adults transition into the big-picture life of the church.

3. The continuing dependence on parents.
    According to Bomar, "Almost 75% of today's 18-to-25 year olds get financial help from their parents."[146]

This is the age group that grew up in the era of *helicopter parents* "who hover over their children and become too involved in their lives, including in college or career decisions later in life."[147] The leading secular expert on the subject of this generation's dependence upon their parents is probably author Ron Alsop, who wrote *The Trophy Kids Grow Up: How the Millennial Generation is Shaking Up the Workplace*. Alsop notes, "What makes these helicopter parents tick? Psychologists find this breed of parent both fascinating and a little disturbing. Some believe that parents don't want to let their children go partly because of their own fear of growing old. High-achieving parents also may consider their child's success a reflection on them."[148] Alsop adds, "Many parents continue to remain vigilant even beyond college, as children apply to graduate schools and enter into the workplace. Hovering, it seems, can be a very hard habit to break."[149]

Churches would do well to recognize and minister to this generation of helicopter parents. It seems as if other cultural organizations utilize the hovering nature of this obsessive, over-protective style of parenting (e.g., public schools, Little League Baseball, community soccer, and even college and university admissions departments). Many of today's parents are very, very involved in the lives of their children long past childhood through college age and beyond. Churches can optimize these relationships by equipping parents to work alongside church leaders and by involving parents in various aspects of ministry. It's critically important to remember that the long-term spiritual maturity for these emerging adults is the mutual objective.

4. <u>The delaying of marriage and changing definition of family life.</u>

   Another cultural shift facing this age group is the seemingly ever-shifting concept of marriage and the family. More and more college-age people are waiting until they earn at least a four-year degree and settle into a career before thinking about marriage or parenthood.[150] In the 1950s, the median age for marriage was 21 years of age; by 2010 that had risen to approximately 27,[151] which means that young adults are waiting later and later to get married. Plus, two-thirds of all twentysomethings currently spend some time living with a romantic partner before they get married.[152] These facts, plus the current cultural and political conversation about homosexuality in the military[153] and the rise in gay marriages,[154] have perhaps influenced a changing definition of family life. It would be somewhat natural to look at these trends and come to the conclusion that families are in trouble and that sin is running rampant in our society. But, maybe we should look at these developments as opportunities to build inter-generational, modeling relationships between older married couples and emerging adults, and to encourage older, Godly widows or widowers to mentor younger adults about the joys and blessings of a true Biblical marriage.

   In fact, this particular point leads us to identify another problem with one-generational programming in adult ministries of the church. Traditional churches tend to separate various age groups of adults into distinct Sunday school classes or adult Bible fellowships instead of developing inter-generational classes where older adults and older married couples could model, teach, and encourage younger adults, including young married couples and singles who are still looking for mates.

5. <u>The growing concern over the economy.</u>
   There's one other cultural trend that has recently affected the vast majority of young adults – and that is the growing anxiety and alarm over national and international economic issues. Many, many young adults, including college graduates, are currently having trouble entering the work force.[155] Maybe this scenario has led to a cause-and-effect relationship regarding pop culture's portrayal of the "slacker" young adults with no career and no goals who are still living in their parents' basement. About 40% of today's young adults move back in with their parents before they start their careers and most go through seven different job changes while still in their twenties.[156] Again this trend could also be perceived by the church as an opportunity instead of a liability.[157] Not only does this period of unsettlement extend the amount of time a church can minister to this age group, it also presents the prospect of challenging them Biblically to consider doing something eternally significant with their lives, which includes providing short-term opportunities for them to serve through the church in the meantime.

In spite of the popular statistics, this generation does not need to be missing in action from the church. As David Kinnaman puts it, "Millions of young adults leave active involvement in church as they exit their teen years. Some never return, while others live indefinitely at the margins of the faith community, attempting to define their own spirituality. Some return to robust engagement with an established church, while some remain faithful through the transition from adolescence to adulthood and beyond."[158] So, what's the difference? I am convinced that we must be proactive about developing and incorporating a strategy to keep them engaged in the church. It begins with the influence of Godly parents, who are committed to a collaborative relationship with church leaders, and includes an intentional transition from the church's youth ministry to adult ministries, and comprises relevant Biblical teaching and opportunities for personal involvement and ownership in their church.

Now let's take a look at how older adults can be involved.

Chapter Nine: Adult Ministry
"Then They Can Train the Younger..."

Upon a recent visit to a fairly large Midwestern church, I took the opportunity to take a walk from their auditorium down the hallway to their "family center" located on the other side of their facility. This structure was indeed impressive. The basketball court was busy with pick-up games at both ends. Another court was crowded with people playing volleyball. Nearby was a busy game room with people hovering around several electronic game consoles, including one active game of *Madden Football* projected onto the large front wall. The coffee shop next door was packed with people, scattered about on various pieces of furniture, drinking coffee.

In some churches you'd think the above scenario must have featured teenagers or college students, but quite the contrary. Everyone in this church's family center was an adult.

In some cases, there seems to be a resurgence of interest in adult ministries in today's church. However, it has been my experience as I visited several churches of various sizes around the country in preparation for this book that many churches emphasize adults to the exclusion of other age groups, or they deemphasize older adults in an attempt to reach emerging generations of younger adults.

Yet, I'm afraid that the same church leaders who would disavow a racially or socially-biased church may in fact be creating a generationally-divided church due to their lack of emphasis on developing a balanced approach to connecting the generations. Even the first-century church had to be instructed to be inter-generational (see Titus 2). It seems, even back then, a growing generation gap was developing in culture and within the church. It's time to shatter that tradition. The church must lead the way on bridging the generation gap. We must teach today's adults to be intentionally and purposefully inter-generational.

In many cases, even within the overall structure of adult ministries, our programs for adults are segregated by age-group distinctions, like young married couples, parents of teens, and seniors. The logic for such programming may have appeared to be sound. On one hand it seems to make sense to build affinity groups around generational distinctives or commonalities such as the age of children or a mutual stage of life. Certainly various age groups of adults have things in common with other people their own age and in their own stage of life.

This was the basic philosophy behind the "young church" or "Gen-X church" movement of creating shared worship experiences for young adults[159] that came into vogue a few years ago. The participants shared the same basic life experiences; they had the same tastes, and often had the same general outlook on life. Even within the overall scope of adult ministries, it made sense to separate people by general age group divisions. So, differing opinions in external trends or fads, such as music and fashion, were solved by dividing the generations into similar age groups.

It's no wonder then that generational consumerism and self-centeredness began to rule the day. It is basic human nature for people to want to have their own way. And so the church moved even closer to an "it's all about me" mentality. The generations who grew up with the old Burger King slogan, "have it your way," began to believe it, and the church adopted the logic of dividing groups of adults along generational lines where people could "worship" along with other people their same age with the same tastes – and the same self-centered, "it's all about me" consumeristic approach to the church.

That's why I say that we must break or shatter that tradition – and it must begin with the adults in the church. Like the Apostle Paul's intent in his letter to Titus centuries ago, we need to teach our older adults today to make intentional inter-generational connections in the church. If not, we'll have churches filled with age-segregated, self-centered, opinionated older adults who don't want anything to do with younger generations. Connecting the generations is essential for the church. Or to paraphrase Brad Powell in his book *Change Your Church for Good: The Art of Sacred Cow Tipping,* if the church is going to carry on, it has to begin reaching out to younger generations."

Here are some simple, yet extremely important steps for teaching adults to be truly inter-generational.

1. <u>Lead adults in learning all they can about younger generations.</u>
   It is very important for church leaders to teach older adults about emerging generations. This includes providing research (putting materials and information about youth and youth ministry into their hands) and giving them exposure to younger people. I highly encourage pastors and other church leaders to motivate adults to be continual students – learning all they can about youth: a vital part of the church of today and the hope for the church for tomorrow.

   It has been my experience that adults will never truly gain an appreciation for younger people if the generations are isolated from each other. Adults must have positive exposure to young people. They must sense the youth's heart for spiritual things and see an active demonstration of their love for Christ and their desire to live for Him.

2. <u>Identify a team of significant adults who are open and willing to change.</u>

In 2007, well-known Christian writer and pastor, Gordon MacDonald penned his widely-read story *Who Stole My Church: What to Do When the Church You Love Tries to Enter the 21st Century.* McDonald gives practical advice to church leaders about how to encourage older saints to embrace the feelings and attitudes of younger believers in the church. In the Preface to the book, MacDonald writes:

> My hope for this book is that it would spark dialogue among people of all generations who love the church. I would be grateful if the book would convince younger generations of church leaders to be more sensitive to the older generation and their thoughts. Conversely, I have a passion that older Christians would be led…to understand why many things about the way we have made the church work must change and reflect new realities.[160]

Again I want to emphasize that this process of changing a traditional church to one that emphasizes inter-generational connections must begin with adults. MacDonald put it very well: churches must adapt to reflect the "new realities" of cultural changes. This does not mean that the Gospel message or Biblical methodologies should change. As the Apostle Paul would say, "God forbid!" God's Word is always relevant and is always applicable. However, it is imperative for churches to identify some significant adults (which I define as people having credibility or influence) who are open and willing to change. Perhaps I am somewhat naïve, but I believe that members of older generations and younger generations alike basically want the same things. They want a church community where they can worship the Lord and grow in Christ as they study God's Word. They also want to see people come to Christ and they want their young people to grow up and go on for God. Simply put, they want their church to go on and be a vibrant witness for Christ long into the future.

Real effectiveness stalls when people become self-centered and when consumerism ("I have to have my own way") dominates. The church must be about Christ – not about individuals getting their own way. That's why I say that it is vital for churches to identify Godly adults who are absolutely committed to the frequent process of reinventing the church so that it will continue to be all that God wants it to be, as Christ tarries, long into the future.

3. Recruit Godly and caring adults to serve as mentors for younger people.
    I will talk more about the concept of mentoring in greater detail later on in this book. At this point, let's suffice it to say that the idea of developing intentional inter-generational mentoring connections in the church is vitally important. Again, an effective mentoring ministry must begin with adults. Godly, committed, and motivated adults can and should develop growing interpersonal relationships with individual younger people to encourage spiritual and personal maturity. The

church should be characterized by a loving community of older adults who are devoted to the concept of raising up future generations of Christ-followers.

4. Build other inter-generational connections throughout the church.

This step seems very, very basic and yet it has proven hard to implement in so many churches. The idea is to take every opportunity possible to connect the generations. It begins with creating an environment where every ministry position is encouraged to include an inter-generational element. The worship team should include people of various generations. The team of ushers and greeters should be comprised of young people and older adults, and so should the audio-visual technicians. Encourage Sunday school and Vacation Bible School teachers to recruit a young person in the church to learn alongside of them. (More ideas for making these connections can be found in Chapter 15.)

5. Develop a plan to identify, train, and utilize younger leaders.

Developing a strategy to raise up a new generation of leaders in the church is also critically important in this process. This will be especially important for members of the Millennial generation who crave involvement and positions of influence. Many researchers have touted Millennials' capacity for leadership and entrepreneurial spirit. One author suggests that "many millennials are rejecting corporate life to follow their dreams. Entrepreneurship may in fact prove to be the perfect career path for the millennials who don't want to end up as 'corporate slaves' and are willing to take risks to marry their talents with their passions." The author goes on to argue that "by starting their own businesses, they can immediately do something personally meaningful rather than wait for a company to give them that chance. They say they want to succeed or fail based on the merits of their endeavors, not the whims of a corporate boss."[161]

Emerging generations want their chance to have influence and to make an impact for eternity. As Thom Rainer puts it, "Millennials are incredibly motivated to make a difference in this world. And they are likely to do so."[162] His research points out that 96% of the current generation believes they can do something great.[163]

The point here is this: get younger generations involved and provide opportunities for them to be involved in leadership in the church. This will greatly help in the transition of reinventing your church for the future.

6. <u>Create a "welcoming community" of adults to help transition teenagers into adult ministries.</u>
   In Chapter 5, I quoted Chap Clark and his idea of a "welcoming community" of adults[164] who are willing to make the commitment to actively seek out and include graduating high school students and then college-age young adults in the world of adult ministries. This too will need to be intentional, or, believe me, it will never happen. As we have already seen, our society has created an

ever-widening generation gap that naturally thwarts an inter-generational mindset. That's why it is so important for the established adults in the church to take the initiative to welcome the maturing young adults into their world.

Youth pastors, youth workers, and parents of teenagers can facilitate this process by identifying Godly and influential adults to serve as a welcoming committee of sorts to make sure that these young adults feel accepted in adult Sunday school classes and other adult programs in the church. I talked to some church leaders that have created a "rite of passage"[165] of sorts in their churches. These "rituals" of transition from adolescence into the adult world include wilderness canoe trips with graduating high school seniors and a team of interested adults, combined youth and adult short-term missions trips, and gender-specific (young men with older men and young women with older women) "Titus 2 retreats." The point of these traditions is for churches to develop an intentional transition between adolescence and adulthood. (See Chapter 13 for more information on this topic.)

7. Implement a thorough whole-church approach to educational ministries.

Another very important action step in the creation of a truly inter-generational approach to youth ministry is the implementation of a consistent educational philosophy throughout all age groups that includes a thorough and comprehensive *scope and sequence*. (I talk more about this concept in Chapter 7.) This approach mandates the development of a church-wide curriculum or total course of study that reflects one sound educational objective for the entire church.[166]

The idea of a church-wide, educational *scope and sequence* was originally popularized via church "Christian education" publishers.[167] (For an example of a publisher's *scope and sequence* as it relates to Sunday school, children's ministry, youth ministry, etc., I suggest that readers take a look at a booklet available in downloadable PDF format from Regular Baptist Press, a "denominational" publisher I served with for several years, at: http://bit.ly/IHsSJg.)

For many years I have taught a seminary course for youth pastors and youth workers on the subject of developing their own curriculum. It's important to note that this emphasis on curriculum does NOT mean just writing individual courses or lessons. It's much more than that. It means having a complete overview of what is being taught (and when) in every educational ministry of the church. I tell my students the only way I know how to do this is to make a chart that includes every teaching ministry in the church – for example, preaching, Sunday school, youth group, small groups, Bible studies, and Vacation Bible School. It also must include a general idea of what spiritual maturity (see Ephesians 4:11-16) looks like and what level of Biblical instruction it takes to achieve that objective.

What I am advocating here is this: it is so important that all of a church's educational ministries are on the same page. There must be one plan from children's ministry, through youth ministry, and all throughout adult ministries. There needs to be one overarching objective (to develop spiritually mature believers) that impacts everything we do in the church. This approach will lead to a consistent philosophy of ministry that helps maturing adolescents move seamlessly into adult ministries. This does not happen in churches that do not have a consistent, overall philosophy of teaching ministries.

8. <u>Actively involve parents throughout church ministries and develop a plan to "adopt" people from the non-nuclear families.</u>

The arena of family ministry is also a key ingredient of any church's ministry to adults. (I'll discuss this subject in greater detail in Chapter 14.) I am convinced that any church can and should give special attention to an equipping ministry that is committed to helping parents be spiritual successes with their children. Of course, this commitment begins with the systematic, expositional teaching of Scripture – which will include an emphasis upon parenting and family life (for example see Ephesians 5:22 – 6:4). This equipping ministry can also include practical parenting classes and other training endeavors that are designed to help Christian parents in the difficult task of raising children. I highly encourage churches to incorporate the stories and examples of older parents who have already "successfully" raised their kids in these training initiatives.

There also must be a balance here. A few decades ago, the term "nuclear families" came into popular use by sociologists referring to what was then the traditional family unit: a father, a mother, and children living in the home.[168] However, over the past several years, the makeup of the family unit has changed dramatically in this country. That definition probably no longer describes the traditional family.[169] Churches in 21st century America now must minister to scores of dysfunctional, weak, and broken families. Plus, as we saw in the last chapter, the number of college-age young adults in this country has grown noticeably over the past several years.

These demographic changes and trends will force the church to examine its strategy and programming for adult ministries. Yes, ministering to families and equipping parents must continue to be a top priority. But, the church must also develop a plan to reach out to people who are not a part of the so-called nuclear families.

Some of the churches I visited have developed a deliberate plan for "adopting" children, youth, singles, divorcees, and other no-familial individuals into other family units so they do not feel isolated and alone within the church structure. Other churches have created programs for specific demographic cohorts. These programs certainly include age-group classes or peer ministries such as children's ministry, youth groups, and college-age ministry.

The important thing to remember here is this – today's ministry to adults must include something for parents and families, and must also feature programming for individuals from non-nuclear family units.

9. Include "singles" and college-age young adults in church programming initiatives.
This brings us to the next important emphasis in effective adult ministry. The largest generation in U.S. history has entered college or is of "college age"[170] – it's time for the church to step up to the plate and make this demographic a top priority (see more about this age group in Chapter 8). An effective ministry to this age group will need a transitional facet to help high school graduates move into the adult world of the church, and it will require some sort of inter-generational assimilation for young adults and older adults.

10. Be proactive in caring ministries and pastoral relationships with all age groups.
A ministry to adults must also incorporate a strategy to provide pastoral care for each individual and each family. Without an emphasis upon caring, your church will have people "fall through the cracks" and ultimately leave the church. This caring emphasis can be accomplished within a small group structure or through a "deacon caring" system,[171] but the important thing is for church leaders to organize a plan for everyone from all ages to be included.

The inter-generational component of a caring ministry is that each person (children, teenagers, young adults, middle-age adults, and older adults) must be included. Romans 12:15 puts it this way, *"Rejoice with those who rejoice; mourn with those who mourn."* An organized caring ministry creates a sense of unity and community within the body that is absolutely imperative for a truly-functioning and Biblical church.

Adults are obviously an integral part of church life, but one generation cannot be the only focus. Other age groups can and must be included in overall body life if a church is to be genuinely inter-generational and all-inclusive in nature. However, as I will emphasize repeatedly in this book, a culture or environment of inter-generational connections in a local church should begin with adults – the established generation with "power" and influence.

Of course, as any veteran youth worker will confirm, the catalyst for lasting change often rests with students. Young people often provide the vehicle and the motivation that can change a culture through their energy, enthusiasm, and idealism. So, be sure to get your teenagers on board and teach them early on about the importance of building significant, influential, and Godly adults into their lives.

Chapter Ten: Senior Adult Ministry
"Even When I am Old and Gray"

"Even when I am old and gray, do not forsake me, my God, til
I declare your power to the next generation, your mighty
acts to all who are to come." Psalm 71:18

I have finally arrived! I'm at the stage of my life when I can proudly display my AARP membership card to receive the discount rate at hotels. My wife and I try to do our grocery shopping on the one day each week that offers the "55-plus-dicount," and I find myself paying more and more attention to those annual Social Security notices. However, I'm going to draw the line by NOT accepting the discount offer for the senior citizen cruise I just received. No offense to anyone (please!), but the last thing I want to do is hang out with a bunch of old people...like me.

Friends, where did we get the idea that it is a good thing for seniors to fellowship and associate only with each other? In fact, I think churches are making a mistake by doing that.

Believe me, I understand. I enjoy being with people my own age. We often share the same memories (remember the good ol' days of the 1960s?), and our values are often the same. We look at life the same way and we have, for the most part, experienced many of the same things. Sure, it makes sense to have friends the same age we are. But, when we transfer that scenario to the church, it may become a detriment to true church relationships, fellowship, and ministry. I am becoming more and more convinced that younger generations need and actually crave healthy and growing relationships with seniors. Today's Millennials seem to relish close, positive relationships with older people. As Ed Stetzer, the president of LifeWay Research observes, "Churched and unchurched young adults are looking for mentors and friends of all ages who have gone through the experiences that they are about to encounter."[172]

This is an incredibly positive cultural phenomenon that pastors and other church leaders must hasten to capitalize on in the church. Not only do today's young people actually appreciate older saints, they can and will learn much from the wisdom, knowledge, and life experiences of older people. That's why it is such a shame for churches to separate the generations almost exclusively in their various ministries and gatherings.

I am a student of today's generational differences. My research and personal experiences have taught me that church leaders will probably need to teach the various generations to begin developing inter-generational relationships. It won't happen automatically. Let's face it – the seemingly ever-widening "generation gap" has permeated our culture for years and years. Churches have "bought in" to this philosophy of separating people by age in most of our educational programming. We hold one-generational classes and socials where the seniors gather in one place, while the young people gather somewhere else. Sure, the various generations gather together during the weekly worship services, but truth be told, the generations have very little to do with each other in most of our corporate services or educational ministries.

So, how do we reverse this trend? I believe it starts with the seniors. It only makes sense that the impetus for developing strong inter-generational relationships begins with the older generation. Our elders have personal life messages that provide a wealth of wisdom and maturity, and our students need their advice and counsel. That's certainly the idea behind the classic Biblical passage concerning inter-generational ministry in Titus 2 where older women were instructed to teach younger women. Our churches' senior citizens must begin to build positive and growing relationships with young people. It may not be easy, but it is the right thing to do. Sure, we get too old to play tackle football, but we don't get too old to be mentors. (Much more will be said about the specifics of mentoring in chapter 11.)

Here are a few simple ways seniors can begin to build mentoring relationships with young people:

1. <u>They should take the time to learn the young people's names and greet them warmly in church.</u>
   I always encourage older adults to take the initiative on this. Young people can and should minister to the senior citizens, but if the seniors go out of their way to speak to the teenagers by name, it is a powerful example of love and encouragement. Of course, the bigger the church the harder it is to do this, but seniors are the ones who have had the longevity of life and the experience to model warmth and friendliness. Believe me, this is contagious – and it sets the pattern for other age groups.

2. <u>They can find time to pray for the church's young people.</u>
   We'll talk more about this later, but it is an incredible example when older people pray specifically for young people. Again, it's important for the older folks to set the example in a praying church. Perhaps the leader of the senior citizens' ministry could secure a list of the teenagers' names and could institute a plan for the seniors to pray specifically for them.

3. <u>They can volunteer to help in the church's children's or youth ministries.</u>
   Since when is it a good idea for the seniors to sit in a classroom exclusively instead of actively serving and ministering? I've always had the view that a church's senior citizens are the ideal people to serve as men-

tors, advisors, counselors, and helpers in the children's and youth departments. Sure, they may not have the health or energy for a full commitment, but what they could give would be very, very positive and edifying.

4. <u>They could invite young people into to their home for a meal, a snack, or cup of coffee.</u>
Older adults often have the time and resources to reach out to younger people through hospitality and the utilization of their homes. This could be a very positive way for seniors to minister to younger people – and it wouldn't require a large investment. I'm convinced that many young people today would love to have these informal and simple times of fellowship and encouragement from older people.

5. <u>They could teach a younger person a "life skill" (e.g., quilting, golf, auto mechanics, or piano lessons).</u>
Seniors often have a life skill that they could teach to a younger person. This capability is often ignored or neglected today, and, as a result, teenagers and young adults are not learning these crafts, hobbies, or skills. My mother is a gifted seamstress and takes the opportunity from time to time to teach younger women in her church how to quilt. My mother-in-law is a skilled musician and has taught piano lessons to young people for several years. We have an inter-generational karate class in our church and several groups of golfers, hunters, and car buffs meet for their various affinity groups regularly. The important thing is for the seniors to take the time to teach these various life skills to younger generations.

6. They should look for opportunities to share their stories.

Today's youth love stories. Most of the recent block-buster movies have been epic tales or stories. God uses human interest, real-life accounts of real people to touch the hearts of others. I think this is the idea behind the truth in Psalm 78:1-8. Older generations were instructed to tell the next generation *"the praiseworthy deeds of the Lord, his power, and the wonders he has done,"* so that *"they would put their trust in God and would not forget his deeds but would keep his commands."* This generation has an affinity for "God stories." Seniors should take every opportunity they can to share what God has done and is doing in and through their lives. Practical ideas abound. Invite young people over to your home and take the opportunity to share your testimony with them. Take a few young people out for coffee. Today's young people love to connect with older people. I strongly recommend that churches use this as a ministry advantage. This simple action step will help break down the generation gap.

The ideas for making basic mentoring connections are almost endless. The important thing is for older people to take the initiative to build and develop positive inter-generational relationships. They are the Godly, older saints with a lifetime of maturity and wisdom. Passing the baton to future generations must be intentional.

According to the U.S. Census Bureau, we live in a country with a dramatically increasing population of older people. At this moment, almost 40 million people in the United States are 65 years of age or older – and that number is expected to grow significantly over the next several years as the Baby Boomers age into their retirement years.[173] It's definitely a ministry paradox to realize that this country's youth population is the largest generation in American history.[174] Many churches are filled with a large number of young people alongside of an escalating number of senior citizens.

Even though most of us have been raised believing there is a considerable generation gap, I believe the different generations in the church need each other and that both sides of the generational divide actually want the same things in the church. Younger people and older people alike desire to serve and worship God in a local church environment that honors God, that teaches and preaches the life-changing Word of God, and that effectively reaches out to the unsaved and unchurched members of the surrounding community with the Gospel of Jesus Christ.

The Bible teaches the unity of the Body of Christ (see Ephesians 4:11-16), and that older people can and should mentor and encourage young people in the church (see Titus 2:1-10). Today's young people need Godly and loving encouragement from the older people in the church, and as we have already seen, this generation of young people is very, very receptive to building close relationships with older people.

It makes sense for older, spiritually mature people to be intentional about personally ministering to younger people in the church. Let's bridge that generation gap!

Ways Your Youth Group Can Minister To Senior Citizens

If you could only do one thing to build your youth ministry's "street cred" in your church, start by ministering to your church's senior citizens! Street cred is contemporary slang for credibility, or for commanding a level of respect. Honestly, friends – this is it! This may be the key to gaining respectability for the youth group in your church. Minister to the senior citizens! The senior citizens have an incredible amount of influence in your church, and to have them as fans of the youth ministry is a tremendous blessing.

I wrote earlier about how the senior citizens can minister to youth. So, in the mode of "turn about is fair play," here are some basic ideas for your church's teenagers to put into practice to minister to the "senior saints."

1. Pray for them.
   It starts here. Motivate your group to pray for your church's older adults – by name! You can obtain a list from the church office or from the senior citizens Sunday school teacher. You'll probably need to remember that some of the key seniors may be shut-ins and unable to attend church very often. Don't forget these people should be the heroes in your church. They've earned your respect for their many, many years of living for the Lord. So, pray for them specifically and let them know that the teenagers are praying for them.

2. Honor them.
   I've talked to several senior citizens recently and they feel somewhat "left out to pasture" or marginalized by the church. This ought not to be. They deserve honor – and it will be highly appreciated if your church's teenagers demonstrate their respect for these older adults. I know several youth groups that host dinners or other times of fellowship for seniors, and that is a great place to start. Let them know they are loved and respected by the emerging generations!

3. Ask them.
   This is a simple idea, but it can be powerfully important. Give them a voice in the church. Your teenagers need to hear from them and need to hear their advice and counsel. There's one especially potent way that you can pull this off. Ask some of your church's Godly senior citizens to share their story or their testimony with the youth. A

131

few years ago, I asked one of the oldest men in our church (a World War II vet) to share his story with our youth group. He was a decorated war hero, and yet he was scared to death by our teenagers. But, when he started telling his testimony, the kids were spellbound. You literally could have heard a pin drop in the room. This simple testimony helped our group connect with him and his wife, and strong relationships developed out of this brief time together. It only makes sense to ask some of your church's Godly and respected senior citizens to share their story with your youth group.

4. Use them.
    I am convinced that you could recruit some of these senior citizens to be youth leaders. Of course, they will all say, "I'm too old." No, the fact is people get too old to play tackle football, but they never get too old to minister to young people. I understand that in many cases it might not work for them to be full-fledged youth workers, but they can and should be involved. Ideas abound from helping with mailings and paperwork, to organizing them into an intentional prayer-warrior team. The point is that these committed older saints can and should be involved. Plus, it will help them feel useful and needed. (Another key idea: recruit them for work projects alongside teenagers. The mentoring effect will be incredible.)

5. Help them.
    Here is one last way to minister to the senior citizens in your church: offer to help them. Your group can help rake leaves, shovel snow, drive them to errands, pick up groceries for them, offer valet parking for them at church, and on-and-on. You will be amazed at how the seniors look positively at teenagers who are servants and

who are helpful to them. This can help your group get their eyes off of themselves and onto the bigger picture of the body of Christ.

The Apostle Paul told Timothy that he could be an example to the believers (see 1 Timothy 4:12). I highly encourage all youth workers to implement these simple ideas to help motivate your teenagers to minister to the older adults in your church.

Chapter Eleven: Mentoring
Being Intentional About Connecting the Generations

I had a dream a few nights ago. (No, it wasn't some inner Freudian wish to give a Martin Luther King, Jr. speech to the masses!) In my dream "senior saints" were actively involved with the teenagers in the church. Some older ladies were showing some of the girls how to quilt. Some of the World War II vets were telling true war stories to the young men who had developed their own battle plans on the latest version of *Call of Duty* video game. The various generations were praying together, laughing together, and sharing their own experiences of what it's like to live for Christ in their own generation. The most amazing aspect of this dream was that there seemed to be a genuine appreciation for each other's music. The teens were gaining an appreciation for the majesty and dignity of the older hymns, and the seniors were learning to listen to the energy and passion of the newer contemporary Christian worship choruses.

Then I woke up...

If the truth be told, this "vision" is more real than I could ever imagine. Maybe it's time to put the brakes on the ever-developing generation gap. Maybe, just maybe, we've got it wrong in the church.

Where did we get the idea that it was wise to segregate the generations? Why are the senior saints in the church library, while the young people are in the basement? Even though I am a fan of many aspects of peer ministry for the reasons identified in this book, perhaps we should be much more intentional about developing growing and loving inter-generational relationships in our churches.

I think this is the idea behind Paul's instruction to Titus for his first century ministry on the Island of Crete as described in Titus 2:3 and 4: *"Teach the older women to be reverent in the way they live...Then they can urge (teach) the younger women"*; and in his counsel to his disciple Timothy in 1 Timothy 4:12: *"Don't let anyone look down on you because you are young, but set an example for the believers in speech, in conduct, in love, in faith and it purity."* Paul made it clear that older people are to teach and encourage younger people – and young people should indeed be examples to other age groups. Believe me, the only way this can happen is if the generations have exposure to each other.

The key influencers here, of course, are parents. Parents must model these relationships in front of their children and they must be willing to encourage their own young people toward developing healthy and constructive relationships with other older adults. My wife and I are so thankful for the ministry other Godly adults had on our own children in the formative years of their lives. We are greatly appreciative of Sunday school teachers, youth pastors, Christian coaches, missionaries, and other Godly adults who cared enough to reach out to our kids. As we talked about earlier, I also love the example of young John Mark in Scripture. He was a young man who grew up in the church (see Acts 12) and who was greatly influenced by other key adults such as Peter, Barnabas, and Paul.

So, how does a traditional church (one that is characterized by generationally-segregated programming) turn its focus toward inter-generational ministry? Friends, I am convinced that it starts with mentoring. Church leaders should do all they can to encourage the older, Godly adults in church to actively and intentionally seek out younger people to mentor. Perhaps the church leaders could be involved in the selection process. Some adults may not have any experience being around young people and may struggle identifying younger people who could use a mentor. It would be wise for church leaders to identify needy young people – maybe those without strong, churched families of their own. However, in actuality, every young person could probably benefit from an older, godly mentor.

The main point here needs to be emphasized. Effective mentoring begins with the potential mentor. Church leaders must encourage and motivate older adults to take the initiative to make the contacts with potential protégés. It is the older generation that needs to give back (to minister to younger people as an investment in the future), and it is the older generation that has the heritage, the wisdom, the maturity, and, perhaps, the resources (at least of time, insight, and discernment) necessary to serve as true mentors. So, this starts with the adults – and make sure that your adult mentors are people who genuinely love the Lord and who are actively living for Him. This is an ideal way for churches to practically engage their older adults in significant ministry as the older folks move into their later years. Remember, we get too old for contact sports, but we don't get too old to minister to kids.

So, encourage your adults to make their first informal, non-threatening conversations with younger people in the church foyer. Adults should introduce themselves and make an initial first connection. As the relationship develops, the adults should begin to ask simple questions that indicate an interest in the young person's life. Questions like: "How's school going?", "What did you do in youth group today?", or "How was the school concert last weekend?" The key here is to show interest in their lives. That's how to begin a growing, personal relationship. Some young people may resist, but my experience has been that the majority of younger people will appreciate any healthy attention shown to them from significant adults.

At some point, encourage the mentors to find some time to pray together with the person they are trying to mentor. I really believe that God will use these brief times of prayer to help this relationship grow into something truly special for each person.

One of the highest hurdles facing a mentoring ministry is the process of carving out enough time to develop a true relationship. I have talked to several adults who feel as if they do not have the time to implement something like this into their schedules. Yet, my take on it is this: "Mentoring is NOT necessarily a commitment of extra time – it is 'doing what you already do,' just doing it with younger people." That's another reason why I love church-based mentoring. These simple, but significant conversations and connections can and should happen at church. You are already there, so why not reach out and attempt to develop a growing and positive relationship with younger people? Maybe my dream will come true.

Not Sitting at the Kids' Table[175]

Remember eating at the kids' table during family gatherings? The adults would sit at the massive dining room table in the big chairs and they'd use the good china, the real silverware, and cloth napkins. But, the kids ate somewhere else, usually on a folding card table, off to the side somewhere, sitting on an assortment of other random chairs and a lone piano bench. The kids would use plastic utensils and would eat off of those ubiquitous Styrofoam plates. There were always two very different tables, with two very different experiences.

It's too bad, but many churches are set up this same way. We've bought into the idea that there is a generation gap and so we've programmed our churches to reflect that.

Friends, it's time to change this paradigm. It's time to connect the generations in your church.

I wholeheartedly believe that real-life, hands-on mentoring is one very practical way that any church, anywhere, can intentionally break down generational barriers – and it must begin with the adults. How many young people do you know who would have the personal confidence or security to walk up to a key adult in the church and ask them to be their mentor? That is not likely to happen very often. Instead, older adults must initiate personal and growing relationships with younger people.

Of course, it is very, very important that you build "guardrails" or safeguards into this process in your church. We live in a dark and sinful world where evil predators and sick people abound. The news accounts are nauseating of coaches, teachers, priests, and other significant adults who take advantage of unsuspecting and gullible young people. Our church just instituted a carefully-crafted "child protection policy," and we are enforcing it with tenacity in all areas of our ministry. I highly recommend that your church leaders do their homework[176] on implementing legal and enforceable guidelines[177] into your church's ministries with juveniles.

However, the sin around us must not thwart the work that our Lord wants to do in and through the various generations in your church. In fact, we all know it's true: when culture is at its darkest – the light of the Gospel of Jesus Christ shines ever brighter! Praise the Lord for His light shining through His people.

Again, it is important to emphasize that effective mentoring is a spiritual exercise and it must begin with Godly older adults. The Apostle Paul outlined the practical ingredients of true mentoring in his memorable letter to the Thessalonian church in 1 Thessalonians 2:8: *"Because we loved you so much, we were delighted to share with you not only the gospel of God but our lives as well."* He made it clear that his relationship with them was based on God's Word (notice his use of *"the gospel"*), but he also emphasized his loving and caring interpersonal connections with them. It's important to note that growing, individual, and inter-generational relationships must include these two imperative ingredients: (1) the Word of God, and (2) sharing your life in a caring and growing manner.

If you are convinced that inter-generational mentoring is the way you should begin to connect the generations in your church, it must be launched through the solid teaching of Biblical truth. Your pastor or other church leaders can use passages such as this one in 1 Thessalonians 2 or the familiar instructions to older women and older men in Titus 2 to challenge your people concerning the development of building inter-generational connections. The Scriptures are also filled with practical examples of people like Barnabas, Paul, and Silas that illustrate how this could work in basic life situations. Perhaps your church could schedule some time within the current structure of your women's ministries and men's ministries to teach your people the importance of mentoring and then launch it within those existing programs. The important thing to remember is that God will always use His Word to challenge and instruct His people, so it is imperative that your church begins this process based upon solid Biblical teaching. I emphatically recommend, based upon passages such as Titus 2, that older women mentor young women and older men mentor younger men. Current culture may teach differently, but this particular safeguard is imperative. Women should mentor women – and men should mentor men!

The next step, practically speaking, is to announce and schedule a meeting for all of the interested adults. It has been my experience that many of your adults will be interested in serving as mentors with younger people. However, I have also noticed that even though adults indicate they are interested in serving as a mentor, they will also feel as if they do not have the time to do it. It is for this very reason that I tell churches that true mentoring is not necessarily an investment of extra time, but it is in fact "doing what you already do," just doing that with younger people.

Over the past few years, I have had multiple opportunities to speak to churches and church leaders about the practical aspects of mentoring.[178] It has been so encouraging to see how personal and inter-generational connections have developed around very basic things. I have witnessed churches where various generations get together around things like golf, quilting, computers, auto mechanics, piano lessons, karate, crafts, and other very simple day-to-day activities. The purpose of mentoring is actually very simple – it is basically the building of growing, inter-generational relationships that foster spiritual growth by just spending time together.

Once a relationship begins in church, the older adult can then invite the young people to accompany them in other non-threatening activities outside of the actual church building. The key is to connect the generations. Practical ideas of how this could work are numerous. Maybe the generations can even sit together during holiday dinners.

Time Flies: Positioning Your Church to Enhance Effective Mentoring

Take a look at Psalm 71:17 and 18: *"Since my youth, God, you have taught me, and to this day I declare your marvelous deeds. Even when I am old and gray, do not forsake me, my God, till I declare your power to the next generation, your mighty acts to all who are to come."* The Psalmist had a passion to *"declare"* the power of God to the next generation. I love the focus of this particular Psalm. Here was someone who had lived for God his entire life – and now in old age, he was incredibly motivated to share "God stories" (*"Your marvelous deeds"*) with the generation to come. This kind of motivation is the heartbeat of truly effective mentoring. This person had a long and beautiful relationship with the Lord of Heaven and his continuing desire was to share his love for the Lord with younger people.

I've personally had the amazing privilege of knowing some people like this. Truthfully, there's not many of them out there (and that's a shame); but the "gray heads" who love the Lord and who enthusiastically want to tell younger people what He has done for them are contagious. This is how good churches are built – it's the joyful expression of Godly older people who love the Lord so much that they can't help but *"declare"* God's faithfulness over the years with the younger, emerging generations.

Have you ever noticed how time flies? My wife and I have been married over 35 years. Our children are all adults and we now have grandchildren. The disasters of 9/11 happened over 10 years ago, and it's been forever since the Dallas Cowboys won their last Super Bowl. (Well, maybe not forever. But, you get my point.) Doesn't it seem that the older we get, the quicker time goes by?

Churches are like that, too. It's also a shame that once vibrant and growing churches are closing their doors in record numbers all across this country. I have had the opportunity to visit some of the churches that were once used of God to launch entire movements that impacted culture, and that once served as models of effective, community-changing ministry. Some of those buildings are in complete disrepair with just a handful of older people huddled together, almost afraid to change in any way. Friends, our churches shouldn't be that way! We must be intentional about declaring God's strength to the coming generations!

How about it? Is your church characterized by older people who contagiously and infectiously share God's wonderful works with younger generations? If not, it should be!

Here are a few quick reminders on how to develop intergenerational mentoring relationships in your church:

1. Be intentional about motivating and training your church's older people to pray by name for younger people.
   This could start by distributing a simple list of names and prayer requests. I've been in churches that encourage older people to develop prayer-partner relationships with younger people in the church. As the

older people pray, the Lord will put a growing burden on their heart for the younger people.

2. <u>Once the older people are praying specifically for younger people, take them on a "field trip" to see the young people in action.</u>
    Paul specifically told his student Timothy to be an *"example"* to older people (1 Timothy 4:12). Yet, how can that happen without exposure to each other? Make sure that your church's older people get to know your young people and see how they are living for God in their own culture. Another way to do this is to give your students the opportunity to serve in significant public settings in your church services.

3. <u>Provide opportunities for the different generations to have intentional, informal contact with each other.</u>
    Some churches ask their young people to host a banquet for the senior citizens and other churches ask the older people to offer to pay for individual students to attend various church youth activities. Other churches schedule informal game nights for the generations to get to know each other better.

4. <u>Once growing relationships have been established, give the generations opportunities to specifically pray with each other.</u>
    Inter-generational prayer can be a real blessing and encouragement, but it can also be rather intimate and perhaps even quite threatening. So, start slowly and see what happens. Ultimately, this can be a powerful and influential force for good in your church. Young people need to hear older people pray – likewise, older people need to hear young people pray.

5. <u>Provide some opportunities for members of the various generations to serve alongside of each other in the church.</u>

   What about your team of ushers or the people in the sound room? And what about your Sunday school teachers? Encourage each serving member of older generations to make it a top priority to recruit a younger person to serve alongside them in their various avenues of ministry. It should be the expected norm in all of your ministries that older people are actively training younger people to take over someday.

Yes, time flies. In no time at all, one generation will pass from the scene and a new generation will be present. God expects one generation to pass the baton to the next generation. Churches must be intentional about doing this or it won't happen.

Chapter Twelve: Graduating From Church?
Helping Students Transition out of Youth Group[179]

Imagine this scenario: It's the first Sunday in September and the classroom seems somewhat empty without the presence of last year's seniors. Obviously, everyone knew they were leaving. The team of youth workers went to graduation ceremonies in June, and several people from the church went to the kids' open-house celebrations. It was fun and quite nostalgic for everyone to look at the old photographs their parents had displayed. Sure, the youth workers knew these kids were leaving the group at some point. Many of them had attended the church since they were little children. But this was the first week they didn't come to the senior high Sunday school class – and they were missed.

The team of adult youth workers reminisced a little bit about each of these kids and talked about what they had contributed to the youth program. Stacy came to everything and always sat in the front. She contributed to every discussion, called visitors, and demonstrated solid leadership skills throughout the ministry. She left early the week before to attend a well-known Christian college. Josh attended Sunday school almost every week, but missed several weeks of the mid-week youth group meetings each year due to his involvement with the school's cross-country and track teams. He is attending a local community college, but no one is sure where—or if—he went to Sunday school or church services that week. Emily grew up in the church along with her two older sisters. No one could recall where any of them went to church when they graduated from high school. In fact, it's sad to realize that they'll probably never see her again either.

I could go on with this fictional story, but the reality is, as I've stated, that the number-one time for people to drop out of church is immediately following high school graduation. The statistics are alarming. Most students who were very active in church and youth group during high school often quit going to church once they enter college.

Current Trends

Our kids *are* leaving the church! As Thom Rainer and San Rainer III point out, "More than two-thirds of young churchgoing adults in America drop out of church between the ages of eighteen and twenty-two. Most of the dropouts leave the church between the ages of seventeen and nineteen."[180]

As I stated earlier, there *is* a missing age group in too many of our churches. Students who were once very active in all that the church offered through its youth ministry are so often leaving church once they graduate from high school. The solution to this situation is more complex than just offering a program or two for college-age young people. Far too many churches are not intentional about helping graduating high school students transition into the overall life of the church. In fact, my observation has been that traditional youth ministry often separates teenagers from other age groups in the church until they leave high school when we kick them out of youth group to forge their own way (spiritually speaking) through their college education, the work force, military service, or other adult responsibilities.

A church must make intentional connections with the next generation, or it will become a one-generation church and slowly decline. That same sentiment was expressed by Gordon MacDonald in his book *Who Stole My Church?*: "Any church that has not turned its face toward the younger generation will simply cease to exist...We're not talking decades – we're talking just a few years."[181]

Why Are They Leaving?

I have spent a great deal of time the last couple of years exploring the causes and solutions for this crisis. My research, reading, experience, and conversations with students, youth workers, parents, and pastors have revealed five significant causes for this exodus from church.

1. <u>Traditional youth ministry is often characterized by separating generational age groups.</u>

   I have been in so many churches where the youth room is literally as far away as possible from where the adults meet. It's almost as if churches don't want the two age groups to mingle at all. Churches tend to isolate the generations along peer lines and the result is often a lack of real, meaningful relationships between teenagers and most adults. It's therefore no wonder when we dismiss them from youth group following high school that they fail to make a positive transition into the adult ministries of the church. Their high school world featured a different program, often a different philosophy of ministry, a different meeting location, different pastors, different musical styles, and very few positive relationships with Godly adults. No wonder they walk away.

2. <u>Many youth ministries fail to build loyalty and ownership to the overall church.</u>

   Youth workers, you'll have to evaluate your own ministry on this one. Are your kids more loyal to the youth group than they are to the church as a whole? As author Robert Laurent observes, "The leading reason why young people leave the church is 'lack of opportunity for meaningful involvement.'"[182] That same idea is illustrated by Steve Wright in his thought-provoking book *Rethink*: "It seems the

147

churches of all denominations and sizes are failing to reach teens with the Gospel and baptize them…If our programs are bigger, our budgets are bigger, our shows are bigger, and our workloads as pastors are bigger, then why are baptisms still declining?"[183]

In other words, we must be intentional about helping our students develop a loyalty and ownership of *their* church. This experience from my own youth ministry provides a tangible illustration of how I learned the importance of this principle. During my early days as a youth pastor, our church hosted a gym night for our teenagers to play pick-up basketball and volleyball. During the evening one of the older gentlemen in our church came into our gym and with his head down walked through our group and down the stairs at the end of that building. In just a couple of moments all of the lights in the gym went out. This dear saint had flipped the electrical circuit breaker. He came back up the steps and was making his way across the gym floor when I stopped him by saying, "Brother, what happened?" He responded curtly, "I turned off the lights." Curiously, I asked, "How come?" This was his rationale: "The teenagers don't tithe, so they don't deserve to use church electricity." Then he abruptly walked out. We got those gym lights back on that evening, but his somewhat misguided logic helped me reevaluate our youth ministry. Were our teenagers tithing? And did they understand the importance of a loyalty and commitment to the overall church?

That conversation helped me see the great value of building loyalty to the church as a whole within the fabric of student ministry. We began to encourage our students to tithe, to get baptized, and to serve within the parameters of the entire church. We taught our young people to participate in church work days, to attend church business meetings, to serve in various church ministries, and to get involved alongside of Godly adults in appropriate avenues of service with children and adults.

3. <u>There may be a lack of clear Biblical and theological teaching in many of today's student ministries.</u>
    Have you ever heard youth workers or other church leaders say something like this? "My teenagers know the Bible. They've heard it all their lives. They need to apply and live what they already know." I urge you to check it out in your group. I recently visited a church where the youth pastor made this claim when I talked with him about the value of materials and curricula: "My students know the Bible," he boasted. "It's a matter of them learning how to live it out." While I absolutely agree with my friend's last statement, I challenged him on the first part of what he said.

    He gave me the opportunity following that morning's church service to meet with a select group of his key students to discern their level of Bible knowledge. I have to admit that this group of students had a basic knowledge of Bible-based facts (for instance, they knew the books of the Bible, they knew about several Bible characters, and they knew some of the general themes of key Bible books). However, they struggled even with a simple understanding of doctrine and theology. Although some of them had strong opinions about some of the basic Bible doctrines, they really struggled knowing how to back up what they believed with Scriptural truth.

Youth workers, we must not ignore the importance of teaching the Bible to our students. My experience tells me that this is a generation that wants to know what they believe and why. (I highly recommend that every church leader read and devour Dr. Christian Smith's classic report on the Millennial generation's religious faith entitled *Soul Searching: The Religious and Spiritual Lives of American Teenagers*.[184] Some of his findings will challenge your thinking and some will almost break your heart.)

4. <u>Many churches are weak in developing spiritual leadership in the lives of maturing teenagers.</u>
   I am afraid that we have been acting as if our teenagers are little kids. So, we try to entertain them and spoon feed them instead of asking them for a growing commitment toward what it really means to follow Christ. I believe that the very nature of youth ministry provides an obvious visual aid of what this idea could look like. I'll phrase it in the form of a question. Do you treat your seniors in high school the same way you treat the freshmen? Doesn't it make sense to think that many of our upper classmen should be more mature in Christ and farther along in their spiritual development than they were as ninth graders?

   We'll talk more about this point below when we get to the solutions, but let's suffice it to say that our student ministries should be places of spiritual growth and maturity that produce senior highers, then young adults, and ultimately fully-functioning and church-active adults who demonstrate a growing commitment to Christ and His church and who live out a maturing influence on others.

5. <u>Too many churches do not intentionally help students transition from youth group into the overall life of the church.</u>

My last observation about why this departure happens is that we are quite weak at helping teenagers transition from their culture of adolescence into the world of commitment and responsibility of adulthood. Not only should churches make ministries for young adults a key ingredient of their overall educational plan, they should also intentionally build sensitivity toward all generations into the framework of their worship and fellowship experiences and programs.

I appreciate the inter-generational emphasis in Gary McIntosh's book *One Church, Four Generations*: "It is crucial that the worship team be intergenerational. The leaders who are seen on the platform influence the people who will attend the service. When people come to a church, one of the first things they do is look around to find people like themselves."[185] He makes a good point. Our churches must be God-honoring places where children, young people, young adults, and older adults alike serve Him and worship Him. It is a shame if churches are willing to overlook or exclude any particular age group.

There are several practical ways churches can bridge the generation gap that exists in so many churches between teenagers and adults. First of all, as I have emphasized throughout this book, I am a huge fan of building intentional mentoring connections in the church where caring and Godly adults seek to develop growing relationships with individual young people.[186] I advocate that this can operate beyond the structure of a typical youth ministry that features a small team of adults who serve as "official" youth workers. Churches can recruit a larger group of caring adults to serve as spiritual mentors for the teenagers. These adults can form positive relationships with kids that will carry over from youth ministry into adult ministry with this by-product: kids will get to know some of the adults on a personal level.

Another way I've seen churches help graduating high school seniors make this transition is through an inter-generational approach to small groups. If your church is working on a small group ministry, why not consider making each of the groups inter-generational in nature? I have seen this to be a very positive thing for the churches when young adults and older adults meet together in small group settings for Bible study, prayer, and fellowship.

Some Possible Solutions

Youth workers, we all must do a better job helping our students transition out of youth group and into the adult ministries of our churches—or help them get actively plugged into a church in the community where they go to college! Our main objective must not be to get them to high school graduation and out of our programs. Instead it must be for them to go on for God for the remainder of their adult lives.

This single chapter does not do justice to this critical topic, but here are a few suggestions to consider as you face the issue of your high school graduates walking away from church once they leave your youth ministry.

1. Equip parents to see the importance of regular church involvement for their children in high school and in college.

   The real issue here, of course, is that if parents see church attendance and church involvement as critically important in their own lives, their children will be more likely to grow up with those same values. However, if parents of teenagers allow work, school, athletic involvement, or other things to come before church, the students will probably grow up with the idea that church is somewhere down the line on the priority list. This doesn't mean that we should be legalistic about not missing even one week of church. Many kids today are busy and I've met several students all across the country who have the ability to juggle the demands of teenage life with a high commitment to Jesus Christ and His church. This just means that we must help our people make a commitment to church involvement because they see it is important to God.

   My parents didn't give me a choice in this. No matter what, church was first. Not the high school basketball team, not a job, not homework – nothing came before our family's commitment to our church. That value stayed with me into college and on into adult life. I don't think it's naïve to believe that emphasis will work today as well. That's why I tell youth workers to equip the parents of teenagers in their youth groups to make church involvement a top priority in the lives of their children now.

Several months ago I met a set of parents who had just dropped off their daughter for an early-admit program at a Christian university a few hours drive from their home. These parents, after hearing me speak about the solutions to the above-quoted statistics about our kids leaving the church, admitted that while they were at the university, they were involved in paying their child's school bill, moving their daughter into her dorm room, helping her select her classes, and even making sure that she had a parking place on campus, but they never took the time to see if there was a good church in that community. Church involvement is a family issue first, and all youth workers should do their best to help parents see the importance of consistent involvement in God's church.

2. <u>Build leadership skills into the lives of your students as they progress throughout their senior high years.</u>
    Youth group must be more than entertainment and a place to hang out with friends. It must be a place of intentional transition from spiritual childhood into God-honoring adult maturity. Simply put, youth group must be a place where high school seniors have more leadership responsibility than ninth graders do. If we want our kids to stay in church after high school, it is very important that we give them increasing levels of leadership involvement as they progress throughout our ministries. Developing student leadership may be more important than we ever realized.

There's another perspective to this matter that I want to share with readers. I have personally talked to several youth workers who told me that they have many senior highers who virtually "check out" of youth group long before they graduate from high school. These students were very active as freshman or sophomores, but became less and less involved as they progressed through high school. Is that happening in your group? Perhaps it is because our youth programs are exactly the same year after year. In some churches, the basic structure of youth ministry is the same for seniors as it is for seventh graders. No wonder kids get bored and quit coming! That's why it is so critical to develop student leadership as students grow throughout our youth ministries. (By the way, I present some specific ideas on this issue in my book *Impacting the Next Generation: A Strategy for Discipleship in Youth Ministry.*)

The solution, of course, is to give your senior highers more and more leadership responsibilities in youth group and in church as they mature. You'll want to make sure that these students are actively living for the Lord so that a lifestyle of carnality and sin is not promoted. However, I really believe that students are much more likely to stay involved in church throughout their college-age years and into their adult lives if they are encouraged to develop specific leadership skills as they progress through their years in your youth ministry. Specifically, I'm talking about giving your older kids opportunities to mentor the younger kids in the group and to be involved in other key avenues of hands-on ministry as juniors and seniors. If churches are going to be proactive about keeping their teenagers in church after they graduate, then it's time to be serious about developing leadership in the lives of maturing students.

3. <u>Develop a genuine loyalty to the whole church, not just the youth group.</u>

   As I said above, I'm afraid that in typical youth ministries, kids are more loyal to the youth group than they are to the church as a whole. If this is the case, it's no wonder that they don't want to be a part of the church itself after they leave youth group. They graduate from high school, we make them leave youth group, and then they struggle to find their place in the larger church community. They don't seem to fit into the adult world of the church, so they tend to feel like the proverbial fish out of water, missing the familiar safety and security of the youth group. Wise youth workers will deliberately ensure that teenagers realize they are a part of the local church as a whole instead of isolating students in the cocoon of the youth group. Ways to do this include providing kids with opportunities for significant ministry, teaching them to give financially (including the discipline of tithing), and giving them positive interaction with people from other age groups. I also recommend that (if at all possible) the church's senior pastor be actively involved in the lives of teenagers. He is their pastor too. Students need to grow up realizing that they are a part of something bigger than their own world of peers.

4. <u>Carefully teach your students the Word of God, including the ability to personalize doctrinal truth.</u>

   Contemporary sociologists and church leaders alike are realizing that college-age young adults are struggling to know what they believe. This is the age when students must come to terms with the importance of clear-cut, rock-solid doctrinal truth. This generation wants to know what they believe. It doesn't matter if they go to a Bible college, a major state university, or enter the military or workforce—these young adults will be forced to evaluate their own personal belief system. They'll ask themselves, time and time again, "Do I really believe this?"

That's why it is so important for our teaching ministries to be much, much more than just quick devotionals we get ready at the last minute. So many youth workers build their teaching times around hot topics of the day or teen-generated subjects instead of the "whole counsel of God" that includes solid Bible content and in-depth doctrinal truth. If we look at youth ministry as a terminal program (i.e., it has a clear beginning and ending), we'll realize that we have a very short amount of time to make sure that our kids are prepared to face an adult world knowing what they believe based on the complete, inerrant, and inspired Word of God.

5. <u>Be intentional about developing wholesome connections between adults and teenagers in your church.</u>
    My last suggestion for youth workers on this subject is something I alluded to in many places throughout this book: the importance of building strong intergenerational connections into the lives of students. We are making a mistake if we isolate teenagers into their own little sub-culture of youth ministry. However, isolation seems to be the prevalent practice of so many of today's youth ministries. Adolescents need and desire healthy and growing relationships with Godly adults. This seems to be the pattern espoused in Titus 2, for instance, as Paul instructed Titus to de-

velop strategic inter-generational ministries in the early church.

Let me be clear, I am not advocating a total departure from peer ministry. I believe in youth ministry, and I can argue for the value of a strong, vibrant church youth program. However, teens need adults and vice versa. The generations will often become very absorbed in their own cultural worlds of friends and experiences if they are not making intentional inter-generational relationships. We must break down generational barriers that tend to develop selfishness around externals such as music, fashion, and other cultural trends.

I wouldn't mind that empty classroom I spoke about in the beginning of this chapter if our team of youth workers knew that Stacy, Josh, and Emily were heartily welcomed into a caring community of believers in an active adult or young adult ABF (adult Bible fellowship) or Sunday school class that demonstrated genuine love and a heart for ministry to and with them. That may be the key to the situation I am describing here – Godly adults who are totally committed to welcoming members of a new generation into the overall life of the church. After all, there is really no such thing as graduating from church!

Chapter Thirteen: Family Ministry
"Continue in What You Have Learned..."

Kids grow up!

This unbelievably profound (I'm being somewhat facetious here) statement sits at the core premise of this book. God wants each one of us to grow up. For example, take a look at Ephesians 4:11-16, especially verse 14: *"we are no longer to be children"* (NASB). The Lord wants His followers to move beyond infancy, both physically and spiritually, to maturity. God's goal for our kids is that they grow through a lifelong process of spiritual development to become more and more conformed to the image of His son, the Lord Jesus Christ (Romans 8:29).

That's why Godly Christian parents and church leaders alike must be on the same page. Through a collaboration of both institutions working together (see Chapter 4), the next generation has the secure fences to grow up and go on living for Him throughout their lives – from childhood into adulthood. Paul's letter to the Ephesian church makes this premise very clear. The church is to be involved in the spiritual maturation process (see Ephesians 4:13-14) and so are Christian parents, especially fathers (see Ephesians 6:4). In other words, it is God's design for the family and the church to work together in an intentional strategy to help the next generation grow in spiritual maturity.

This substantiates the idea that a balanced view of youth ministry is essential for the church. It was never God's intention for our kids to remain as adolescents. He wants them to grow up into adulthood and go on for Him – and that's why the collaborative influences of the home and the church working together for the common goal of on-going spiritual maturity are so important.

There are, however, differing views and opinions within evangelical Christianity today on how the family and the church could and should work together. One source of research and information concerning these various viewpoints is *Perspective on Family Ministry* by Paul Renfro, Brandon Shields, and Jay Strother (edited by Timothy Paul Jones).[187] This book contains some very interesting comments from different perspectives relating to family ministry. One of the most helpful aspects of the book is the chart on page 52 that outlines the different models of family ministry. The following characteristics are identified:

Programmatic Ministry Model:

"Ministries are organized in separate 'silos,' with little consistent inter-generational interaction. 'Family ministry,' when it exists, is one more program. The program may provide training, intervention, or activities for families. In scheduling programs, churches may deliberately seek to be sensitive to family's needs and schedules."

Family-Based Ministry Model:

"Church's programmatic structure remains unchanged, but each separate ministry plans and programs in ways that intentionally draw generations together and encourage parents to take part in the discipleship of their children and youth."

Family-Equipping Ministry Model:

"Although age-organized programs and events still exist, the church is completely restructured to draw the generations together, equipping parents, championing their role as primary disciple-makers, and holding them accountable to fulfill this role."

Family-Integrated Ministry Model:

"The church eliminates age-segregated programs and events. All or nearly all programs and events are multigenerational, with a strong focus on parents' responsibility to evangelize and to disciple their own children."[188]

It's interesting to take a look at the varying ways churches tend to approach their ministries toward families and parents. The traditional approach to youth ministry seems to reflect the *Programmatic Ministry Model* where age groups are virtually segregated from each other throughout the spectrum of church ministries. For example, teenagers often receive their own specialized educational training, their own style of worship, and often have their own pastors. At the other end of this continuum is the *Family-Integrated Ministry Model* where peer ministry is practically abolished in favor of family units meeting together for mutual training, worship, and where parents, especially fathers, are trained and encouraged to be the only influencers over their children.

As I mentioned in Chapter 5, one of the most vocal leaders of the *Family-Integrated Ministry Model* is Voddie Baucham, preaching pastor at Grace Family Baptist Church in Spring, Texas,[189] and the author of *Family-Driven Faith*. Baucham observes that "the family-integrated church movement is easily distinguishable in its insistence on integration as an ecclesiological principle." He goes onto explain, "Our church has no youth ministers, children's ministers, or nursery. We do not divide families into component parts. We do not separate the mature women from the young teenager girls who need their guidance. We do not separate the toddler from his parents during worship. In fact, we don't even do it in Bible study."[190]

Another influential source that has sparked a great deal of conversation and discussion about this particular approach is the relatively recent movie *Divided*,[191] produced by Christian filmmaker Philip Leclerc. This documentary asserts that modern youth ministry is actually contrary to Scripture, and that it has its roots in Darwinistic evolutionary thought. Discerning readers and viewers will need to draw their own conclusions about this model of ministry. (For a balanced and honest evaluation of this movie, I recommend that you read the review of *Divided the Movie* by youth evangelist Greg Stier in the November/December 2011 issue of *Group Magazine*.[192])

Let me be clear on this point because it is so important. I wholeheartedly believe that parents are to be the primary influencers over their children (for example, see Deuteronomy 6:1-9). I also believe that God has instituted His church to exist to help bring Christ-followers to maturity in Christ (for example, see Ephesians 4:11-16 and 2 Timothy 3:11-17). That's why I emphatically want to emphasize that even consistent Godly parents are not to be the *only* spiritual influencers upon their children. I must confess that I have personally talked to Christian parents all over the country who do not allow their children and teenagers to attend the church's Sunday school or youth groups out of some arrogance or misguided impression that the church will negatively affect their kids. The two Biblical, God-established institutions (the family and the church) must work together for the common goal of our kids going on to spiritual maturity. I'll discuss some of the key questions surrounding this issue in further detail below.

My own personal conviction is that there must be a collaborative effort between these two God-ordained institutions for the long term spiritual success of the next generation. A balance must be struck between these two above-mentioned extremes of how churches relate to families. I have already made the case in this book that a total segregation of the generations in the church is a huge mistake. It is also important to note that I am not a fan of the *family-only* philosophy of ministry for a variety of Biblical and practical reasons. Some of which I will outline in this chapter.

There is an initial question that must be addressed. Does the Bible advocate teaching everyone of all ages at the same level of educational instruction? And is it really wise to teach everyone of all ages in the same environment at the same level of instruction? In other words, do children, youth, and adults learn alike, or should the church and Godly Christian parents seek to work together somehow for the common goal of helping emerging generations grow to spiritual maturity?

A Premise of Growth and Development

I believe that the Bible is clear on the basic premise that children and adults are distinct and that those age groups have differing levels of personal and spiritual maturity. Take a quick look at the principles identified in the following passages:

-Various age groups are identified as distinct – Psalm 148:12

-Young men and old men are different – Proverbs 20:29

-Children were exempt from paying the temple tax – Matthew 17:25-26

-Jewish parents took 12-year olds to the temple in a significant rite of passage – Luke 2:41-42

-Children have immature thinking and reasoning development – 1 Corinthians 13:11

-God does not want us to stay as children – Ephesians 4:14

-Older Godly women are to teach younger women – Titus 2:3-4

-Olden men and women are different than younger men and women – Titus 2:1-8

-People of different ages are to be treated differently – 1 Timothy 5:1-2

-Children, young men, and fathers were identified separately – 1 John 2:12-14

By inference, there seems to be a definite Biblical precedent for the importance of teaching specific age groups at a level they can understand, and within a structure where they can grow and develop spiritually. I also honestly believe that age-segregated ministry (e.g., children's ministry, youth ministry, and adult ministry) partially came to such wide-spread acceptance out of a genuine desire to help the age groups learn and mature at their own appropriate learning levels. From a personal perspective, I spent several years of my professional ministry life as an editor of church youth materials, and I have first-hand experience in developing age-appropriate educational materials for use by church youth workers in Sunday schools and youth groups. It was certainly our motive to help students develop a personal grasp of the Scriptures in a way that could be applied to their day-to-day lives.

Again, a balanced approach is in order here. Parents and churches, working in harmony with each other for the spiritual good of the next generation can and should provide suitable learning and growing educational and training opportunities and experiences in a format where children, youth, and adults can learn and grow at their own levels. To put this another way, churches must balance youth ministries alongside of intentional and growing inter-generational connections.

My argument for a balanced approach to youth ministry (balancing peer ministry with strong inter-generational connections) is also seen in the Biblical concept of basic growth and maturity. Take a look once again at the opening sentence in this chapter, "Kids grow up!" Scripture is filled with references to the fundamental idea of personal and spiritual maturation. God never intended our offspring to remain children – He intended them to grow up. Practically speaking, that thought is prevalent throughout the Bible. God wants us to grow up.

Several years ago, during a routine visit to a local children's hospital to visit a young man from our church, I mistakenly entered the wrong room and met the family of a child who was either eight or nine years old and who hadn't grown in any area beyond the size of an infant. That heart-wrenching event gave me an incredible visual aid of how sad it is when there is no growth. This is true physically, and it's also true spiritually. God expects growth. His goal for His children is that we grow through the process of becoming more and more like His son the Lord Jesus Christ (again see Romans 8:29).

There's another very practical visual aid in life that provides an apt illustration for this priority of growth and development. Each of us is born into our own individual families and God certainly uses parents to facilitate growth – physically, emotionally, and spiritually. However, it has never been God's intention that children should remain with their parents throughout their entire lives. In fact, the Scriptures say, *"a man will leave his father and mother"* (Genesis 2:24, Matthew 19:5, Mark 10:7, and Ephesians 5:31). Yes, parents are to be the primary spiritual influencers upon their children, but ultimately our kids will grow up into adulthood and live on their own. So, the goal here is adulthood and maturity. As Ephesians 4:14-16 puts it, *"We are no longer to be children...We are to grow up in all aspects into Him"* (NASB).

That grand mission is best accomplished through the shared efforts between consistent Godly parents and a Biblically-based local church.

The Role of the Church: Providing Spiritual Examples

What then is to be the role of the church in this process of developing spiritual maturity? Among other things, the church exists to provide Godly, spiritual examples of what it means to genuinely and actively live for Christ. (For a fuller understanding of the different purposes of the church see Rick Warren's *Purpose Driven Church*.[193]) The Bible is full of real-life illustrations of what this looked like in the early church. Older people were seemingly actively involved in the lives of younger people (see Acts 12:1-17 for an example of an inter-generational prayer meeting), and the reciprocal was also true – the Apostle Paul specifically instructed his disciple, Timothy, to be an example to older people in the in church in 1 Timothy 4:12: *"Don't let anyone look down on you because you are young, but set an example for the believers in speech, in conduct, in love, in faith and in purity."*

The Scriptures also contain multiple explicit imperatives about this idea of living as an example in front of other believers. Here is a brief list of some of those mandates:

> 1 Corinthians 11:1 *"Follow my example, as I follow the example of Christ."*

> Philippians 3:17 *"Join with others in following my example, brothers, and take note of those who live according to the pattern we gave you."*

> 1 Thessalonians 1:6-7 *"You became imitators of us and of the Lord; in spite of severe suffering, you welcomed the message with joy given by the Holy Spirit. And so you became a model to all the believers in Macedonia and Achaia."*

> 2 Timothy 1:13 *"What you heard from me, keep as the pattern of sound teaching, with faith and love in Christ Jesus."*

> 2 Timothy 2:2 *"And the things you have heard me say in the presence of many witnesses entrust to reliable men who will also be qualified to teach others."*

2 Timothy 3:14 *"But as for you, continue in what you have learned and have become convinced of, because you know those from whom you learned it."*

The early church got it. They understood the importance of developing Godly and growing inter-generational connections. The idea of being an example is quite clear in Scripture.

A Real Life Illustration – The Story of John Mark

For one illustration of what this looked like, let's take another quick look at the life of young John Mark. Again I encourage you to read Acts 12 and 13. Take the opportunity to identify from the text some of the people who specifically impacted his life during those formative early years. The people of the church met in his home for prayer – certainly members of the body of Christ provided multiple examples for him. His parents opened their home for the church to gather, so undoubtedly his parents were significant. The Apostle Peter showed up following his miraculous escape from a martyr's prison. Later on, Peter declared himself to be John Mark's spiritual father (see 1 Peter 5:13), and the early missionary team of Barnabas and Saul took him along on the first missions trip ever. Several people invested in his life and served as spiritual examples for this young man who grew up in the church.

The story, of course, continues with some bumps along the way. Acts 13:1-13 tells the account of how John Mark quit the missionary team and went back home to Jerusalem. This departure ultimately caused a major dissension between Saul (soon to be Paul) and Barnabas (see Acts 15:36-41). But, you know the rest of the story. John Mark didn't end up as a quitter. In fact, at the end of his life, Paul wrote that John Mark was *"helpful to me in my ministry"* (2 Timothy 4:11).

John Mark's Godly parents, the body of Christ in the Jerusalem church that gathered for prayer in his home, the Apostle Peter (who himself knew what it was like to bounce back after failures), the hard-liner Saul/Paul, and his uncle (some translations use the word for cousin or relative) Barnabas (see Colossians 4:10), all played significant roles in his early spiritual development and all were undoubtedly used of God to help propel this young man into a life of profitable ministry where he would ultimately serve as the human author of the Gospel of Mark.

The Role of Parents: Providing Consistent Models

We've discussed the role of the church in the spiritual growth and development of young people; now let's take a further look at the role of parents in that process. Unquestionably, parents are to be the primary influencers upon their children, as I have previously stated. This should be accomplished through an intentional strategy of *"training and instruction"* (see Ephesians 6:4), which certainly implies a deliberate plan of "nurture and admonition" (which is the phrase used in the King James Version). In other words, successful parenting requires systematic guidance and effective discipline.[194]

Did you notice the words I used in the last paragraph – *intentional, deliberate,* and *systematic*? Parenting definitely requires careful and purposeful responsibility – and yet, so many parents take it so lightly and so haphazardly. In fact, a report from the Barna Group research organization revealed that 85% of Christian parents believe they are primarily responsible for the spiritual development of their children, but very few parents spend *any* time during the week interacting with their children on spiritual matters.[195] Most parents responding to their survey had no intentional plans for their children's spiritual training. That attitude is far removed from the Biblical concept of parenting as presented in passages such as Deuteronomy 6:4-9 and Ephesians 6:4.

That brings me to what I believe is the key to effective Biblical parenting – parents with genuine, consistent, and *unfeigned* or un-faked faith. For clarification of this idea, take a look back at what may be the clearest explanation of true Biblical parenting in Deuteronomy 6:4-9.

I understand that some Hebrew scholars see a collective focus in this passage on the entire nation of Israel. They say that the language in the text is plural and could apply to the culture as a whole and not just individual parents. Their point is that the familiar commands presented in this passage were given to the community at large instead of specific parents, and gave the larger nation a hands-on responsibility with the next generation.[196]

As I mentioned in Chapter 3, the Bible expects parenting to be an intentional strategy where one generation loves the Lord *"with all your heart and with all your soul and with all your strength"* and then lives that relationship out in specific ways in front of the next generation. Notice that the language in this passage indicates that this transfer takes place as life happens (*"impress them; talk about them; tie them"*). Parents were to make their relationship with God the top priority in their lives and then utilize the various situations in life to purposefully and systematically teach and show their children to love Him that way, too. The key here was the consistency of the parents. Their genuine faith can't help but be transferred from generation to generation.

In the New Testament, the classic human illustration of genuine faith is vividly portrayed in Paul's description of Lois and Eunice in 2 Timothy 1:5 where Paul writes, *"I have been reminded of your sincere faith, which first lived in your grandmother Lois and lived in your mother Eunice and, I am persuaded, now lives in you also."* Timothy's grandmother and mother were amazing visual aids of that genuine, sincere, real, or un-faked faith – and Timothy caught it, too. Twice in that one verse it says that Timothy himself possessed *genuine* faith. It was real in his life as well.

A Real Life Illustration – The Story of Timothy

So, what can Christian parents do to help their children grow up and go on for God? I'm convinced that we must look to the Scriptures for the answers. In the pages of the New Testament we are told the stories of some young people who grew up before our eyes (so to speak) in the Biblical narrative and who continued to live for God long into their adult lives. One of those young men was Timothy. We meet him in Acts 16 as a young man growing up in church and we read his story throughout the Epistles, including Paul's last letter to him in 2 Timothy. There are many things in the Bible that we can learn about Timothy, but for the sake of this chapter, let's take a look at some of the things his parents (especially his mother, Eunice – see 2 Timothy 1:5) did right.

It's important to note that parenting is never a formula or a recipe. It doesn't work to frivolously think that a few quick ideas lead to spiritual success with our kids. However, if we look at the sweeping principles that seemed to guide this family, we can take away some very practical advice for raising our own kids for God today.

1. A consistent lifestyle (2 Timothy 1:5).
    Probably the most obvious thing that this family did right was Eunice's and Lois's consistent or genuine walk with God. The Bible calls theirs an *"unfeigned"* (KJV) or un-faked faith! Timothy's mom and grandmother demonstrated a genuine relationship with God – and it impacted Timothy. Notice again in verse 5 that Timothy also demonstrated a genuine faith. He grew up and went on for God – and that's what we want from our kids, too.

2. Communication of God's word (2 Timothy 3:15).
    The second thing this family did right was that they made it a priority to communicate Biblical truth. Notice that from his earliest days, Timothy learned the Scriptures. The next two verses (2 Timothy 3:16 and 17) reveal that this strategy was much more than rote memorization of the Text. He also learned that Biblical principles are *"profitable"* for life and that these principles lead to true spiritual maturity.

3. Collaboration with the church (Acts 16:1-5).
    There's another key element to their strategy that is worth identifying and that is their cooperation with the church to help develop Timothy's faith. Acts 16 identifies him as a *"disciple,"* who as a young man already had a good testimony with the other believers. He also was personally selected by the Apostle Paul to go along on this missionary journey. The text expounds on the purpose of their ministry: *"So the churches were strengthened in the faith and grew daily in numbers."* Obviously, the church was a priority to young Timothy. He grew up in church and committed himself to a church-based ministry.

4. Concern for people and culture (Acts 16:1-5).
    The Acts 16 passage also presents an interesting scenario of Timothy's circumcision even though he was a Greek (see verse 1). He perhaps was willing to submit to this cultural ritual due to the cross-cultural background in his own family. This somewhat dysfunctional family environment undoubtedly produced a heart-felt concern for other people and a genuine sensitivity for others.

5. <u>Commitment to ministry (Acts 16:1-5).</u>
The final positive thing I'd like to identify from this family was their dedication to God's work. They were willing to allow their son to follow Paul along on this journey. Without any visible hesitation on anyone's part, Timothy joined the missionary team and set off on what was the beginning of his call to vocational ministry.

Timothy was a young man who grew up and went on for God. The narrative of Scripture points out some identifiable things that helped in this process. Perhaps there is practical wisdom here for today's Christian families to implement into the fabric of raising their own kids.

I love how the Apostle Paul admonished his readers in Colossians 2:6: *"So then, just as you received Christ Jesus as Lord, continue to live in Him, rooted and built up in Him, strengthened in the faith as you were taught."* We want our kids to grow up and go on for Him. So does God!

Two Important Questions about Ministering to Parents Families:

What should the church do to help weak, ineffective, and dysfunctional families?

According to a statistical overview of recent news reports: (1) the divorce rate in America hovers around 50%; (2) the typical age for people getting married has risen from around age 22 to almost age 29 in a short period of time; and (3) fewer and fewer people are choosing to get married at all.[197] Added to that is the recent political conversations about the rise of same-sex marriages in the United States.[198] There is also ample anecdotal evidence out there to substantiate a claim for a propensity for unhealthy and dysfunctional family units. I don't think it's much of a stretch to say that the institution of marriage in popular culture is in deep trouble.

Churches ministering in today's culture will need to address the new normalcy facing the traditional nuclear family.[199] However, this trend must not release the church from its Biblical imperative to *"equip"* (Ephesians 4:12) for *"the work of ministry, for the edifying of the body of Christ"* (NKJV).

I am a long-time advocate of the church developing an intentional strategy for building up solid, healthy, and God-honoring families. This will require training, education, and a purposeful plan to develop inter-generational mentoring relationships between older "successful" parents helping and encouraging new, younger parents. Parenting is too important to leave this process to chance – especially when a simple approach of connecting the generations could proactively solve the problem of younger parents not knowing what to do.

I also believe that churches can and should develop and institute a strategy where healthy, strong parents could "adopt" children and teens from weak, dysfunctional families. Again, this point illustrates the importance of the church providing intentional, inter-generational mentors for kids from these weak and unhealthy family situations.

The answer to this question clarifies the practical importance of an effective and Biblically-based local church youth ministry – not because youth workers supplant the Biblical authority and responsibility of parents, but because there will be many, many non-traditional families within today's culture. I think this is idea is exemplified in passages such as James 1:27, *"Religion that God our Father accepts as pure and faultless is this: to look after orphans and widows in their distress and to keep oneself from being polluted by the world"* and Acts 6:1-7, Romans 15:26, Galatians 3:28, and Colossians 3:11. The Biblical ideal for the church is that it should reach (Mark 15:16), include, welcome, and minister to everyone.

Are parents the best (the only) disciplers of their children?

As Scott T. Brown, the author of *A Weed in the Church* and the director of the National Center of Family-Integrated Churches,[200] emphasizes, "Scripture teaches that the discipleship of youth should be directed by parents and oriented around the family's day-to-day activities." He lists the following Biblical passages in support for his overarching claim: Deut. 11:18-19, Acts 10:24, Romans 16:5, 1 Corinthians 16:19, Eph. 6:4, Col. 4:15, Philemon 1:1-2, and 2 Timothy 1:5.[201]

Certainly these verses contain some general support for the role of the home in the life of believers. However, I believe it is quite a stretch to cite these particular references as proof texts for a true Biblical model of discipleship. Some of the references listed here refer to the basic responsibilities and roles of parenting and others speak of places when the early, first-century church met in the homes of believers.

I want to reemphasize that I unequivocally believe that parents are to be the primary influencers on their children – and this definitely includes training, education, and spiritual development.

Yet, it is important for us to remember here that the primary Biblical pattern of true discipleship happened outside of the home and family structure (see Matthew 28:19-20, 2 Timothy 2:2, and 2 Timothy 3:10-11). Biblical examples of discipleship include Christ with His disciples and the Apostle Paul with men such as Timothy, Silas, and Luke. (One excellent source that identifies and explains the Biblical model of discipleship is Robert Coleman's work, *The Master Plan of Evangelism.*[202]) This intentional educational method required a great amount of teacher-to-student time with each other and directly followed the rabbinical ideal of students following and learning from hands-on teachers (see Luke 4:40, "*...everyone who is fully trained will be like his teacher*").

In Christ's classic treatise on the cost of discipleship in Luke 14:25-27, the Lord told His followers, *"If anyone comes to me and does not hate father and mother, wife and children, brothers and sisters – yes, even their own life – such a person cannot be my disciple. And whoever does not carry their cross and follow me cannot be my disciple."*

This may sound very harsh, but the truth is that sometimes family entanglements actually get in the way of true discipleship. It has been my experience after having served for several years as an administrator and faculty member in Bible colleges, that in some cases even well-meaning Christian parents stand in the way of their children serving on the mission field or in full-time vocational ministry. In other situations, I've known people who aren't willing to follow God's call or leading in their own lives due to the excuse of handling family responsibilities. It sounds callous and harsh, but it does happen – quite often in fact. Families can, in fact, hinder and thwart genuine spiritual growth.

I am absolutely convinced that the New Testament clearly presents the crucial collaboration of parents and the church being actively and intentionally involved in the spiritual development of children (see Ephesians 4:11-16 and Ephesians 6:1-4). Parents, especially fathers, must take the Biblical responsibility to teach and train their children spiritually. Likewise, the church must equip believers to serve the Lord and educate Christ followers toward spiritual maturity. The partnership of these two institutions working together for the spiritual growth of the next generation is a powerful and life-changing influence.

Chapter Fourteen: Changing the Paradigm
From Age-Segregated to Inter-Generational Churches

A "paradigm shift" is a change from one way of thinking to another.[203] This concept came into vogue over the past few years in the business world, usually signifying a transformation from one method of doing something to another and it usually implies a substantial shift in the way the culture thinks and operates.

Throughout history there have been several transformations in the basic *modus operandi* – or mode of operation – for the church. As an illustration of what I'm talking about let's consider the meeting facilities for the local church. According to the New Testament, the first century church often met in people's homes (see Acts 12:12 and 1 Corinthians 16:19 for examples), while shortly thereafter there seems to be historical evidence that the church began to meet in synagogues and other public buildings. It wasn't very long after that when the church began to construct its own meeting sites,[204] and centuries later the paradigm or normal procedure for the church in most cases (at least in Western culture) is still for the church to have its own building. Overtime, the shift actually became tradition.

As I highlighted in the early chapters of this book, another paradigm shift took place in church history that has become the traditional course of action for most churches even now in the 21st century. Of course, I am referring to the age-segregated model of one-generational (or even multi-generational) churches. A walking tour of most traditional churches today (see Chapter 1) will certainly reveal our inclination to almost totally separate the generations for most church functions and ministries.

Friends, it's time for another paradigm shift! It's time to develop an intentional balance of peer ministry (e.g., children's ministry, youth ministry, and adult ministry) with inter-generational ministry (e.g. mentoring, prayer, and other intentional connections) in the church. Yes, a balanced view of connecting the generations is essential for the church!

So, how can we change the paradigm from a traditional church to a truly inter-generational church? In this chapter I will present a series of simple, yet essential steps for affecting lasting change in your church. I'd ask you to visualize the old illustration of slowly turning a large ship.

Here is how one author on the subject puts it:

> If you had a ship full of passengers and you knew that for the people's sake the ship needed to be going in the opposite direction, how would you change course to ensure that most of the passengers would still be riding together in the ship on this new course?...If you turned the ship all at once to go the opposite direction, the ship would capsize and there would be a lot of people lost at sea. If on the other hand the risk of any casualties made us too scared to even attempt to turn the ship around, then it would be just a matter of time before the passengers would die off one by one with those remaining forgetting even why they were on the boat in the first place.
>
> The only alternative for us to turn an existing age-segregated church into one that was age integrated was to turn it slowly. Turning the ship slowly would allow for three things. First, due to the fact that the ship was indeed turning, we would ultimately arrive safely at our desired destination. The ship would still be intact. Second, people would not be thrown overboard because of the ship's gradual turn-

ing...Third, for those who refused to go with us in the opposite direction from all of the other ships around us, they would have plenty of time to lower themselves down in the lifeboats and wait for one of those ships to take them in.[205]

There is wisdom in changing traditions gradually and there is great value in bringing people along this process slowly but surely. The most important feature of this change in your church's basic method of operation is your absolute belief in the reasons for making this shift. Remember, that this book is not advocating "throwing the baby out with the bathwater" (that seems like a bizarre analogy anyway), nor am I promoting the idea of swinging pendulums in going from one extreme to another (I'll address that concept more in the next chapter). We're talking here about developing a balance of peer ministry AND inter-generational youth ministry. It is imperative that we remember that this balance is much needed and completely essential. The traditional church with her age-segregated methodology is not working – nor would the complete departure of peer ministry be wise (or even Biblical) due to the importance of helping people grow and develop in Christ at their own level of learning and maturity.

So, before we take a deeper look at HOW to make this change, here are some key reasons WHY this change must be made.

1. <u>A Biblical conviction of the importance of developing healthy and growing inter-generational connections.</u>
   To affect real change in the church we must be absolutely convinced of the Biblical imperative to connect the generations. Our convictions must be based on the Scriptures. I have listed some of the Biblical passages elsewhere in this book that confirm the importance of one generation reaching and impacting the

next generation. Perhaps the clearest presentation of the generation-to-generation principle in Scripture is the listing of the genealogies in the Biblical text. For example take a look at the genealogy of Jesus in Matthew 1:1-17. This particular list traces the generations from the patriarch Abraham through the Messiah. It's important to note that this directory not only charts the human family line of Jesus, but it is also a historical overview of the entire nation of Israel. Not only was the generation-to-generation principle clearly emphasized within family lines, it was also a significant priority within the whole historical account of the Lord's chosen people. The Jewish culture understood the importance of working together (national leaders, teachers, and one family to another alike) for the common goal of seeing the next generation grow up and go on in their faith.

2. <u>The epidemic of young adults leaving the church following active youth ministry years.</u>
    It's time to get serious about this issue. David Kinnaman, the president of the Barna Group research organization, argues, "We are at a critical point in the life of North American church; the Christian community must rethink our efforts to make disciples. Many of the assumptions on which we have built our work with young people are rooted in modern, mechanistic, and mass production paradigms." He goes onto explain, "We need new architects to design interconnected approaches to faith transference...We need to rethink our assumptions."[206]

He's right. We must change the way the traditional church has done youth ministry and instead develop an intentional plan to connect the generations. Although there are many, many positive aspects to our conventional and now long-established patterns of youth ministry (see my list of those attributes in Chapter 7), the devastating practice of totally separating the generations has reaped the catastrophic result of young adults walking away from actively living out their faith and their involvement in church following their years as teenagers in the youth group.

It *is* an epidemic. The multiple sources of research (as quoted in this book and highly-publicized elsewhere) shout the facts – kids who were once plugged into church are leaving in droves. Of course, there are exceptions. I have personally visited churches of various sizes who are doing things well and who are doing things right. I can confidently state that almost invariably these success stories (where kids are going up and going on for God) are churches that are deliberately and purposely working hard to develop strong inter-generational relationships. As I have emphasized throughout this book, young people who have healthy, growing relationships with several significant Godly adults, including their parents, are much more likely to stay active and engaged in church as they grow and mature into adulthood.

There is one caveat, however, that deserves our attention here. No matter what the circumstances are, we must champion the unmerited and life-changing grace of God. We have all known real-life examples of young people from incredibly dysfunctional families and from weak, traditional, and run-of-the-mill churches who miraculously commit to a life of whole-hearted devotion to Christ. We must praise

God for the amazing testimonies of kids, who in spite of very difficult personal difficulties and situations find the God-given strength to commit to a life of dedication and consecration to Him. In other words, raising the next generation to live totally for Christ is never a formula or pattern. It's only by His grace that He saves us and that any of us grow up to go on living for Him.

3. The goal to develop a balance of peer ministry alongside of inter-generational youth ministry.
    The third reason I must highlight for making the change to a balanced approach is our own personal belief in the goal to change the paradigm. That belief must be rooted in Biblical convictions and must be based on our desire to be a difference maker in the church. Traditional youth ministry isolated the generations. We pulled teenagers out of the established programming in the church with a desire to be relevant to the developing youth culture and to teach youth at their own level of learning and understanding. Both of those ideals were implemented with very positive intentions and sound motives. Our youth ministry forefathers wanted to reach young people for Christ and wanted them to learn how the Scriptures applied to their lives within their own world. However, these objectives soon morphed into the isolation of generations. The teenagers had very little connection with influential adults, other than, in some cases, their parents, and a very limited team of committed adult youth workers. The general population of teenagers in most churches has not developed very many positive relationships with adults – and the adult ministries of the church have not generally included teenagers or pre-teenagers. We've made a

mistake. It's no wonder our kids are walking away. We have inadvertently created a "church within a church" mentality where our youth groups are nothing like "big church" and our emerging generations do not have any real connections with members of older generations.

Our goal must be to change this scenario – and the way to do that is to develop and introduce a balanced approach to youth ministry. The commitment to turn the ship is essential. Yet, let's not overreact. To quickly restructure our programming toward a complete departure of peer ministry will lead to chaos in the church. Most likely our teenagers and younger children will hate it, and parents with children and teenagers are likely to drift away to other churches with more traditional age-group based ministries. If we leave things as they are (mostly one-generational or multi-generational programming), we have surrendered and given up the fight to change the paradigm. As a result, the next generation will continue to leave the church once they are out of high school and on their own.

As Albert Einstein reportedly said, "The definition of insanity is doing the same thing over and over again and expecting different results."[207] It's time to shatter our traditions. This is an epidemic, and the lives and souls of emerging generations are at stake. We must be Biblical in our approach and it is absolutely essential that we intentionally connect the generations in the church.

How to Change from Age-Segregated to Inter-Generational
Once we are convinced that we must make this change we'll need to develop a strategy to implement this essential bal-

ance in our church programming structure. Here are some simple, yet very important action steps for you to consider:

1. <u>Pray and search the Scriptures.</u>
   This process, like any aspect of our ministries, must begin by taking the time to bathe our intentions and plans in prayer. Of course, it is also essential to be totally positive that our methodologies are firmly rooted in the Bible as well. It's not enough to have good intentions or ideas – and it is dangerous to adapt humanistic and culturally-based techniques to make them work in the church. I'm all in favor of being culturally sensitive and I am very, very thankful that God's plan did not include "cookie-cutter" churches. Even a cursory reading of the New Testament reveals a wide spectrum of how churches operated within the basic structure of *ecclesiology* that is developed in the Scriptures. It's obvious in the book of Acts that the Antioch church did not look like the Jerusalem church. (See Acts 2:40-47 for a description of the church in Jerusalem and compare that with the overview of the church in Antioch in Acts 11:19-30 and Acts 13:1-3.)

   We must base the polity of our ministries on the clear teaching of the Bible and we must have a doctrine of the church that is Scriptural. However, it is interesting that within the New Testament's Epistles there are a wide range of generalities that give us the liberty of "doing church" differently from other churches as long as we base our methodologies soundly upon what is there.

   To illustrate this point, it is clear that the New Testament office of *deacon* is specifically mentioned in the

Bible (see Philippians 1:1 and 1 Timothy 3:8-13 for examples), but there are no obvious instructions in the Epistles that specifically outline what deacons are to *do*. Some look at Acts 6:1-7 as an illustration of how deacons are to function in the church, but there is debate among Bible scholars if this particular passage is meant to describe the office. John MacArthur makes this statement regarding deacons: "The question arises as to whether these seven can be properly viewed as the first official deacons, and forms of the Greek word *diakonos* (deacon) are used to describe their ministry (v. 1-2). Yet to view them in terms of a formal office is anachronistic."[208]

I'm convinced that the Bible allows and illustrates a certain level of creativity and adaptation in the way individual local churches can be structured. But, it is imperative that we operate our churches with the clear confidence and conviction that our message and methodologies are firmly based on what God wants us to do.

2. <u>Motivate and train your church's leadership team.</u>
True change will require a team of Godly and influential leaders that are committed to implementing a balanced inter-generational approach in the church. Lasting change will demand much more than a "lone ranger" who rides into town with a personal agenda to "fix" all of the ills in the church. Real leaders understand the importance of recruiting a team of other leaders around them who can ultimately expand their influence.

I'll make this very personal. Once you have finished this book and if God puts a growing burden on your heart to affect change in your church, you will need to recruit a team of other influencers who will be able to increase your own personal level of influence within the church. If you are the pastor, begin with other key leaders. If you are a youth pastor, begin with your team of volunteer (lay) youth workers. See how this works? The important thing is to recruit, then motivate and train, a team of other leaders around you who are willing to actively implement an inter-generational philosophy within your church – or at least within your specific area of influence (more about this later).

3. Establish a church-wide inter-generational philoso-phy of ministry.
    You'll need to do your homework on this one. Let's make the basic assumption that you are convinced of the essential nature of inter-generational youth ministry. This is only the beginning. Now comes the hard part; you will now need to go through the exacting and challenging process of teaching your church about the importance of developing intentional inter-generational connections. Begin, of course, with the Word of God. Take every opportunity to teach your people the Biblical priority of connecting the genera-tions in the church. God will always use His Word to change hearts. Plus, it's critically important to estab-lish the Biblical base in a public manner before trying to institute a change in philosophy in the church.

    Teaching publically on the importance of inter-generational ministry is a great way to set the stage for a slow, but intentional implementation of select inter-generational connections. Beginning informally can be more powerful than a total shutdown of existing programs only to recreate some other programming structure in an attempt to be inter-generational.

I visited a church that had just recently implemented the *family-integrated church* model of ministry.[209] This church did away with their Sunday school and all other age-segregated programming in lieu of church-wide movement toward a family oriented philosophy of ministry. They promoted the *family-integrated* idea and they touted their plan for families to sit together and meet together throughout every ministry of the church. As I interviewed this pastor, however, he did admit to offering a nursery during their weekly Bible study time and he acknowledged that some of his lessons had to be "given in a simple way" in order for the younger people in the audience alongside of their parents to understand what was being taught. I'm sure this pastor was well-meaning and well-intentioned in his motives. However, he didn't last very long in that church and upon his departure, the church immediately returned to a traditional structure of ministry.[210] I came away from the interview with the direct impression that this pastor went about the process of changing the structure of their programming way too quickly – and he did not implement a balanced approach to generational ministry.

4. Equip parents to be a spiritual success with their own children.

As I emphasized in Chapters 4 and 13, Godly parents have the God-given responsibility for the upbringing of their children. As any parent knows, raising children is a daunting responsibility – and it is very hard work. The church can minister effectively to parents and family members by equipping parents for God-honoring and effective parenting. Of course, each local church will have attendees and members from dysfunctional and un-Biblical families, and churches will need to provide programming and resources for people of all ages who attend from these family units.

The key to helping parents be a spiritual success with their own children is to establish a plan to equip parents in basic, Biblical parenting skills. Notice what MacArthur says about this idea of *equipping* as found in Ephesians 4:12: "[Equipping] basically refers to that which is fit, is restored to its original condition, or is made complete. The word was often used as a medical term for setting of bones."[211]

Pastors can do themselves a huge favor by systematically *"perfecting"* (KJV) or equipping parents of young children in an attempt to help them see and implement their God-given responsibility to *"bring them up in the training and instruction of the Lord"* (see Ephesians 6:4).

5. <u>Start slowly – begin by asking significant older people to begin the process.</u>
As I mentioned above, it is very, very important to start this process slowly. However, I'm not talking here about "tortoise speed" where the progress in indistinguishable and unnoticeable. In other words, get started!

I highly recommend that you begin with your church's significant older people. These seniors may need to be encouraged, challenged, and taught to build intentional relationships with young people, but it behooves you to start with them. They have long-term credibility and an integrity that comes from their many years of living faithfully for the Lord.

It will be important to identity which specific people to involve and then meet with them to encourage their involvement. It's critical that you begin this step by asking your seniors to begin the process by praying specifically for individuals from emerging generations by name. God will use their prayers to put a growing burden on their hearts to become actively involved in the lives of younger people. Once this happens you'll be able to suggest specific ways for them to make connections that will develop growing relationships with young people.

6. Get emerging generations involved.
    Once the senior citizens and other influential older people are on board, it's time to get younger people involved. I'll mention several specific ideas to make this happen in the next chapter, but the important thing here is to encourage your young people to take specific actions to reach out to other generations in your church.

    Remember that the theme of this chapter is *changing the paradigm*. Real change usually begins slowly and is implemented over time. Lasting change happens most often when young people begin to do practical things toward a specific goal. In other words, as you motivate your church's younger people to become proactive about making inter-generational connections, they'll grow up with the idea that those connections are the normal and usual way of "doing church." They will be much more likely to continue to develop inter-generational connections once they become adults.

7. Begin intentional mentoring.
    Chapter 11 gives some practical advice on how to implement the concept of mentoring into the fabric of your church. I suggest you reread that chapter and perhaps take a look at a simple booklet I wrote of the subject entitled, *Mentoring the Next Generation: A Strategy for Connecting the Generations*.[212]

    I define mentoring this way: an older Godly adult taking the initiative to develop a personal, growing relationship with individual younger people to encourage spiritual and personal maturity. So, the key is to put the elements of this definition into practice in your ministry.

8. Expect inter-generational serving.
    Here's another very practical idea that will help expand the inter-generational mindset of your church. Expect every ministry involvement to include an inter-generational distinctive. In other words, make sure that everyone who is serving in any capacity in your church understands that they should recruit someone younger to work alongside of them. There should be members of various generations in the worship team, your ushers should feature young people serving with other people, teachers should recruit and train younger "junior" teachers to learn from them, etc. This should be the expected norm in your church. Each and every ministry position should somehow include an "older-teaching-younger" approach.

9. <u>Be consistent about building total church loyalty.</u>

For the past several months I have served on the constitution revision committee in our church. We are working hard to change the basic mentality that relates to what it means to be a church member. Historically and perhaps culturally, I'm afraid we have equated church involvement to showing up for services most weekends. Somehow we have communicated the idea that church loyalty means attending the worship and preaching services. We're trying to raise the bar in our constitution to make church membership more like the New Testament pattern. We're doing this by including wording that indicates that a commitment to church is much more than just showing up. It requires a personal relationship to Christ, a desire to grow spiritually, a willingness to serve and give financially, and a habit of fellowship with other believers. As we have focused our attention on what it truly means to be a church member, our committee has realized that these ideals should be true of young people as well as adults. Our people of all ages should know Christ as personal Savior and should be growing in Him. We want them to actively serve the Lord in the various ministries of the church and they have the obligation to give financially to support church initiatives and programs. Plus, they should demonstrate a lifestyle of joining with other believers in times of fellowship.

I share this illustration from my church to emphasize that churches desperately need a total-church philosophy of ministry instead of one emphasis for adults and different areas of emphasis for youth. If you want to change the paradigm in your church to an inter-generational model, this consistency across age groups is absolutely imperative.

How to Influence Your Church Even if You Are Not in Leadership

I encourage you sometime to take a look at a video on *YouTube* entitled "Derek Sivers – How to Start a Movement."[213] It's a popular and oft-viewed look at some basic principles of true leadership. (You can also read a transcript of this video at: http://sivers.org/ff.) One of the most interesting quotes in this trendy little film is the statement, "One of the best ways to start a movement is to show others how to follow…When you find someone doing something great, be the first person to stand up and join in."[214]

Friends, it is possible to change the paradigm in your church even if you are not the lead pastor or a member of the pastoral staff. It is possible to "start a movement" without necessarily being *the* leader or being in charge. The point is that anyone can have influence by simply making the commitment to make this work. Use whatever influence you have to model inter-generational connections. Take every opportunity you can to build inter-generational relationships and encourage others in your age group to do the same. If you teach a Sunday school class or lead a small group, use that forum to integrate the generations. You can even use your own home as a launching point. Be sure to follow the safety principles as outlined in this book, but get started.

It is possible to break traditions and change paradigms!

Chapter Fifteen: Caution – Swinging Pendulums
Don't Throw the Baby Out with the Bathwater

"Don't throw the baby out with the bathwater" – it's somewhat of a bizarre expression to be sure. Supposedly this idiom has its roots in ancient German literature where an artist's simple illustration showed a woman throwing a baby out with waste water. The saying suggests the avoidable error of eliminating something good when trying to get rid of something bad.[215]

Let's apply this expression to basic church structure. Over the years something that was originally designed to reach members of the emerging youth culture with the Gospel and to effectively minister to a booming number of teenagers in this country has become cumbersome, traditional, ineffective, and perhaps even a grave mistake. History now gives us a certain perspective that our youth ministry forefathers didn't have. They indisputably wanted to do something culturally relevant – they wanted to reach kids for Christ. So, a strategy to keep teenagers relatively isolated from other generations was born. Their intentions were positive and admirable. But, this decades-old experiment was intrinsically flawed. It hasn't worked to keep our young people completely separated from other age groups. They seemingly enjoy this approach as adolescents, but they don't recognize the value of this segregation when they reach adulthood. As a result, our kids are walking away from church in droves, often because they don't really know anyone in the adult world of the church. The separation of youth from adults has turned into a liability.

But, that doesn't mean that we should now swing the pendulum totally away from the overwhelming advantages of a strong youth ministry (see Chapter 7 for a list of some of those advantages). Sure, this discipline has its weaknesses, but its strengths are incredibly valuable – and they are worth maintaining. We must not overreact.

Readers, let's **not** throw the baby out with the bathwater!

Instead of swinging the pendulum away from a positive church emphasis on youth ministry, let's strike a balance. Let's balance the many Biblical and practical advantages of youth ministry along with a commitment to intentionally involve older generations in the lives of the next generation. It's essential that we develop and institute a complete church-wide philosophy of ministry that has the same basic approach for teenagers as it does for other age groups. A church's youth ministry may look and sound somewhat differently than its adult ministry, but the basic approach and structure must be the same. The objective (to develop spiritual maturity for a life of commitment to Christ, see Ephesians 4:11-16) and the means to reaching that objective must be the same across the various ministries and age groups of the church.

The pendulum must stop in the middle. We must strike that balance. It's essential for the current and future health of the church. Our churches need healthy and Biblically-based youth ministries AND our churches need strong, healthy, and growing inter-generational connections. That's the balance.

Making Inter-Generational Youth Ministry Work
So, how do we make this idea of inter-generational youth ministry work in a specific local church setting? Here are some basic ideas to put into practice in your church.

1. Recruit select significant adults to serve as youth workers.

The most customary level of adult-to-youth connections in the church is the obligatory team of adult youth workers who are assigned the task of running the church's youth ministry. Let's start here. It's probably safe to make the assumption that most traditional churches, at least in Western culture, have one or more adult youth worker allocated with the grand task of ministering to teenagers. Actually, this is an incredible way for select adults to build strong relationships with young people. My wife and I are very appreciative of the caring and committed adults who served as youth workers when our children were teenagers and active in our church's youth groups. I also personally served as a youth pastor and then a youth worker for many years in the churches where our family was involved, and I greatly enjoyed the opportunity to build quality relationships with several different teenagers. The point is that the church's "official" youth workers can and will develop strong connections with youth, be it via a paid, professional youth pastor or through a team of volunteer or "lay" youth workers. These faithful youth workers have the ability to build into the lives of emerging generations and can truly impact their lives for Christ on into adulthood. However, this is just a starting point. There must be other levels of intentional inter-generational connections.

2. Utilize adult-led small groups.
   Another way to involve adults in the fabric of church youth ministry is through adult-led small groups. Here's how one youth worker describes his small group ministry:

We wanted to have more adults involved...We accomplished that goal by giving them the ministry. On Wednesday night, I'm not the guy on stage who is funny/wise/spiritual/ everything-a-teenager-wants-in-a-youth-leader. I'm the announcement man. I get up, pray for the night, make the announcements, and then send them off to small groups after some praise and worship. That's my job. Remember: I'm the youth minister. To the untrained eye it might seem like I've taken a back seat. In reality, I've given 10-12 adults more say in the youth ministry on Wednesday night than would have been possible under any other format.

Each night, somewhere between 3 and 10 students meet with their small group leader for 30-45 minutes. They laugh, they play, they learn about one another, and then dive into the Word of God. If we were bigger and bigger, these adults would serve as chaperones. They'd watch kids come in, break up the fights, then make sure they left at the right time. They'd talk on some level before and after, but in reality, they would miss the huge ministry they have right now. The great thing is, on Wednesday night, there isn't one youth minister in the room. There are at least 10. Having these men and women lead in the youth ministry in a big way means that...the Body of Christ is coming together to serve His church.[216]

This youth worker explains it well. Small groups allow other youth workers to get involved in the lives of individual young people. I'm not going to present a primer on how to do small groups here. There are tons of resources out there on how to develop and implement a small group element in youth ministry. If you want to incorporate small groups in your ministry, I highly suggest that you do your homework. Read the books and articles and talk to other youth pastors and youth workers who are already committed to this strategy before you begin this emphasis. The important thing to think through is this: an adult-led small group ministry provides specific and tangible ways for dedicated adults to build real and lasting relationships with young people.

3. Develop intentional mentoring connections.
    As I have repeatedly emphasized throughout this book, mentoring is an ideal way for churches to develop another layer of healthy inter-generational relationships. Today's teenagers are craving adult mentors and scores of youth ministry specialists are now touting the need for launching an intentional mentoring ministry.[217] I am convinced that a truly effective mentoring ministry begins by challenging the Godly, motivated, and caring adults in your church through the Scriptures to take the initiative to develop constructive, growing, and spiritual relationships with younger people. As I have frequently told churches around the country as I have presented this concept to them, mentoring is not necessarily a commitment of *extra* time; it is doing what you already do, just with younger people. I also believe that the best mentoring anywhere takes place at church, and perhaps begins in the church foyer with caring adults going out of their way to meet, greet, and build growing relationships with young people. Mentoring can be very, very successful in an adult-to-teenager

197

relationship, but it can also be developed with the church's overall adult ministries with older adults being intentional about developing connections with younger adults (e.g., older widows with young divorcees and older parents helping young parents).

4. <u>Expect and motivate inter-generational ministry opportunities.</u>
    Another very effective way of developing an inter-generational emphasis throughout your entire church is to create a culture where it is expected (almost re-quired) that every ministry position (Sunday school teacher, usher, sound room technician, children's ministry leader, etc.) is supposed to recruit and train a younger person or persons to work alongside of them in their specific avenue of service.

    This principle should be especially true in the most visible and public ministries of the church. Let's use the church's worship team for example. I referenced him earlier, but I agree with Gary McIntosh from Biola University when he argues, "It is crucial that the worship team be intergenerational. The leaders who are seen on the platform influence the people who will attend the service." McIntosh goes onto as-sert that "when people come to a church, one of the first things they do is look around to find people like themselves. The people on the platform communi-cate a tacit message about who attends the church, so...care must be taken to have people of all ages up front."[218]

    I also think it is imperative for a church that wants to build inter-generational connections to especially re-cruit younger people to serve alongside of adults as greeters and ushers. It's often true that perception is reality. As McIntosh so eloquently alluded, it is essential for the church to publicly demonstrate an inter-generational emphasis. Plus, the natural side effects of younger people serving and learning alongside of adults are powerful, habit forming, and life-changing.

5. Provide ways for adults to share their stories.

    Today's Millennials love and relate very well to stories. A recent post on a blog about marketing and branding describes this generation well: "Millennials think in images, the 'language of story-telling'...Millennials remember stories, not facts. Stories provide an opportunity where facts don't."[219] It's no wonder that the world of this generation is dominated by social media websites such as Facebook. It's also very revealing that many Millennials do not hesitate to publically share very personal information on these sites knowing this cyberworld is actually being accessed by adults as well.

    Emerging generations connect with adults who are willing to share their stories – warts and blemishes as well. Churches can utilize this interest in stories by providing planned and spontaneous opportunities for older adults to share their stories or testimonies with younger generations. I referred to this story earlier, but several years ago I asked one of the oldest men in our church to tell his story to our teenagers. He was a World War II veteran who flew bombing raids from Great Brittan into France and Germany following the infamous D-Day invasion. I'll never forget the reaction of our group. The teens were captivated. They were hearing a real-life version of *Band of Brothers* or *Saving Private Ryan*. This vet's 15-minute testimony had lasting results in our church. The teens were moved by his story of drama, but also by his spiritual and emotional conflict as a result of the bombing of innocent people. Their loving connection with him and his family lasted for several years after that one testimony time – and it motivated us to take other opportunities for seniors to share their stories with our group.

Ways to incorporate these stories into your programming are quite endless. You could invite significant adults to take a few moments to share their testimony in Sunday school or youth group meetings. Time could be allotted in the church worship services periodically for this purpose. Informal fellowship times could be scheduled for the various generations to gather and a group facilitator could be used to motivate the participants to share their stories in an allotted amount of time before something else is scheduled. Homes could also be utilized for this specific purpose. You'll be amazed at how powerful these simple "story times" can be for your church.

6. <u>Create occasions for viable inter-generational fellowship and socials.</u>
   This idea follows on the heels of the previous point. I highly recommend for churches to become purposefully inter-generational in the scheduling and organizing times of fellowship and interaction. Church "pot-luck dinners" tend to be notorious for being either one-generational or multi-generational in nature (see my definitions and descriptions in Chapter 5). Parents dutifully gather their young children to eat with them, teenagers are likely to gather with other

teenagers, and older adults sit with other older adults in almost predefined affinity groups. Church leaders must be intentional about turning these events into occasions for developing inter-generational connections.

Some churches host banquets or dinners for the youth group to host the church's seniors. Other churches schedule "board game nights" in the church's family room where people of various gen-erations can gather around tables just to play games together. The ideas here are basically endless as well.

7. <u>Supply tangible means for positive exposure to other generations.</u>

I appreciate the Apostle Paul's challenge to his stu-dent Timothy in 1 Timothy 4:14: *"Don't let anyone look down on you because you are young, but set an example for the believers in speech, in life, in love, in faith and in purity."* It's amazing to me that young people can *"set an example"* for other believers. They can – but, it won't happen without specific times of exposure to the other generations. The generations must have contact with each other. Being an example requires exposure. Again, this is why it is essential for the church to develop growing and lasting inter-generational connections.

Readers can figure out what ideas would work in your church. The important thing is to plan and schedule regular times for older generations to have positive exposure to younger generations and for younger generations to have affirming exposure to older generations. It's amazing how generational dif-ferences and tastes quickly fade into unimportance and insignificance when the various generations connect and have positive and constructive exposure to each other.

From Youth Group into "Big Church" – Adults Taking the Initiative to Welcome Younger Generations

The real key to developing a genuine inter-generational youth ministry is for adults to create the "welcoming community"[220] that my friend Chap Clark talks about his book *Hurt: Inside the World of Today's Teenagers*. It is up to you, of course, to determine what that community looks like in your church. However, it is imperative for the adults to begin this process. Teenagers certainly can be encouraged, motivated, and taught to build relationships with adults, but lasting change in the culture of your church will depend upon the adults (including the current leadership structure of your church) to be on board with this as a top priority.

I also want to revisit one other statement made by youth ministry guru Chap Clark, and that is the importance of helping our youth develop strong relationships with five significant adults.[221] There's a wealth of research that also reveals how important it is for kids to have healthy, strong personal relationships with Godly and caring adults. This may in fact be the most important and practical solution to the epidemic of kids walking away from church following high school. Younger people are much more likely to stay engaged in church if they have genuine, unwavering, and growing relationships with at least five significant and Godly adults.

Lasting church effectiveness tends to get damaged by the blunt force of swinging pendulums. Throwing the baby out with the bathwater is not the answer. We'd be dumping something very good in our drastic attempt to change the paradigm. The answer is not to do way with youth ministry and all other forms of peer ministry. The long-term solutions are to develop an essential balance in programming and to be intentional about connecting the generations.

Conclusion

We began our journey together through this book on a fictional walk around the church; so let's continue our tour. Along the way the paradigm has changed. This time Godly and faithful adults from the oldest senior citizens to young married couples and young adults are actively engaged with the children's and youth ministries. The educational and worship ministries of the church have become inter-generational in nature. The teenagers are actively involved in various church programs and are utilizing their gifts and abilities in serving the Lord in the church. Devoted, caring adults are serving as mentors, teachers, and disciplers for members of emerging generations. Parents and other family members are committed to working in harmony with church leaders to help their kids grow up and go on for God. Children, youth, and adults are committed to learning and applying Scriptural truth to their own lives and are passionate about reaching out to others.

It looks like the church is being what it is supposed to be. The journey continues.

"To Him be glory in the church and in Christ Jesus throughout all generations, for ever and ever! Amen" (Ephesians 3:21).

APPENDIX:

MY BASIC PHILOSOPHY OF YOUTH MINISTRY

The church's mission is to produce spiritually mature believers who are prepared for a life of service for Christ.

- **2 Timothy 3:10 - 17:** *"You know all about my teaching, my way of life, my purpose, faith, patience, love, endurance, persecutions, sufferings – what kinds of things happened to me in Antioch, Iconium and Lystra, the persecutions I endured. Yet the Lord rescued me from all of them. In fact, everyone who wants to live a godly life in Christ Jesus will be persecuted, while evil men and impostors will go from bad to worse, deceiving and being deceived. But as for you, continue in what you have learned and have become convinced of, because you know those from whom you learned it, and how from infancy you have known the holy Scriptures, which are able to make you wise for salvation through faith in Christ Jesus. All Scripture is God-breathed and is useful for teaching, rebuking, correcting and training in righteousness, so that the man of God may be thoroughly equipped for every good work."*

- **Ephesians 4:10 - 17:** *"It was He who gave some to be apostles, some to be prophets, some to be evangelists, and some to be pastors and teachers, to prepare God's people for works of service, so that the body of Christ may be built up until we all*

*reach unity in the faith and in the knowledge of the Son of
God and become mature, attaining to the whole measure of
the fullness of Christ. Then we will no longer be infants,
tossed back and forth by the waves, and blown here and there
by every wind of teaching and by the cunning and craftiness
of men in their deceitful scheming. Instead, speaking the truth
in love, we will in all things grow up into him who is the
Head, that is, Christ. From him the whole body, joined and
held together by every supporting ligament, grows and builds
itself up in love, as each part does its work."*

MEANS TO REACH THAT OBJECTIVE (2 TIMOTHY 3:10-17)

1. **Systematic teaching of God's Word (v. 10 "teaching"):**
   Creative, systematic teaching of the Bible is foundational for
   spiritual growth to maturity. It is the Word of God that
   changes people's lives – for salvation (Romans 10:17 "...*faith
   cometh by hearing, and hearing by the Word of God*") and for
   spiritual growth (2 Timothy 3:16 17).

2. **Modeling of spiritual maturity (v. 10 "way of life"):** Students need to see the reality of a personal relationship with
   Jesus Christ lived out in adults. Qualified leaders need to be
   discipled for leadership training (2 Timothy 2:2 2 Timothy
   3:10 14) – and needy students need growing, personal inter-
   generational mentors (1 Thes. 2:8).

3. **Everyday application of Biblical principles (vs. 10 - 13 " continue in what you have learned and have become convinced of"):** Believers will only grow towards spiritual maturity as they have the opportunity to live out Biblical principles in everyday life (Acts 16:3 *"Paul wanted to take him along on the journey."* See also James 1:22).

4. **Parental influence and family support (v. 15 "...from a child thou hast known the Holy Scriptures."):** Reinforcement in the home is essential for real spiritual growth and maturity (Deuteronomy 6:1 - 12). However, God's Word offers real hope for change even for those from "dysfunctional" families (2 Timothy 1:5, Acts 16:1).

MEANS TO REACH THAT OBJECTIVE (2 TIMOTHY 3:10-17)

- We must get God's Word into the hearts minds of our students.

- We must equip Godly adults (youth workers, mentors, parents) to model Biblical truth in front of their students.

- We must provide relevant application of Biblical principles into everyday life experiences via balanced, life-related activities

- We must do whatever we can to support parents and families as they seek to raise their children for the Lord.

Mel Walker...

...is a talented communicator, both in speaking and writing skills, who has been greatly used of God to impact thousands of lives for over 35 years of specialization with teenagers and youth ministry. He is the co-founder and president of Vision For Youth, Inc. – an international network of youth ministry that exists to train and encourage youth workers and students for effective ministry. After serving as a youth pastor for several years in southeastern Michigan, he taught youth ministry courses and served in various administrative roles at Faith Baptist Bible College in Ankeny, Iowa, and Baptist Bible College & Seminary in Clarks Summit, Pennsylvania.

Mel then ministered at Regular Baptist Press in Schaumburg, Illinois for almost 10 years as director of student ministries. In that role he led RBP in the complete revision of their junior high and senior high youth materials. Mel is also the author of several books on various topics related to youth and youth ministry – including *Pushing the Limits: Unleashing the Potential of Student Ministry* (published by Thomas Nelson) and *The Greenhouse Project: Cultivating Students of Influence* (published by Word of Life) – which he co-edited with Mike Calhoun. He also wrote 3 booklets on general themes of youth ministry – *Impacting the Next Generation, Mentoring the Next Generation*, and *Reaching the Next Generation* (published by Regular Baptist Press).

He has organized and led several national and statewide youth events and he speaks to thousands of teenagers, parents, youth workers, and church leaders both nationally and internationally at camps, conferences, retreats, and youth events each year. He is a graduate of Baptist Bible College & Seminary in Clarks Summit, Pennsylvania (A.A., B.S., and M.Min.) and has done additional graduate studies at Faith Baptist Seminary and Iowa State University.

Mel and his wife, Peggy, have three adult children (all of whom are active in vocational ministry) and three grandchildren, with three more on the way. They currently live in northeastern Pennsylvania and are active in various ministries and leadership roles at Heritage Baptist Church in Clarks Summit, Pennsylvania.

He was also recently named as Vice President for Enrollment External Relations at Baptist Bible College & Seminary in Clarks Summit, PA.

Mel Walker
Vision For Youth, Inc.
PO Box 501
Chinchilla, PA 18410

mel@visionforyouth.com
www.visionforyouth.com
www.intergenerationalyouthministry.org
www.melwalker.org

Note to readers:

More information from Mel on the subject of *inter-generational ministry* can be found on the following web site:
www.intergenerationalyouthministry.org

This additional information includes PowerPoint slides from the author's training seminars on this topic and the full set of workshop notes and interactive projects for church leaders. The slides and notes are available free of charge for the readers of this book. A one-hour video of Mel presenting some of this material is also posted on the web site.

Mel is available to present this material in a variety of settings for pastors, youth pastors, parents, and other church leaders. For booking information contact him directly at: mel@visionforyouth.com.

Bibliography

Alsop, Ron. *The Trophy Kids Grow Up: How the Millennial Genera tion is Shaking Up the Workplace.* San Francisco, CA: Jossey-Bass, 2008. Print.

Anthony, Michael J. (editor). *Introducing Christian Education: Foundations for the Twenty-First Century,* Grand Rapids, MI: Baker Academic, 2001. Print.

Arnett, Jeffrey Jensen. *Emerging Adulthood: The Winding Road from the Late Teens through the Twenties.* New York: Oxford, 2004. Print.

Bainbridge, David. *Teenagers: a Natural History.* Vancouver: Greystone, 2009. Print.

Barna, George. *Transforming Children into Spiritual Champions.* Ventura, CA: Regal, 2003. Print.

Baucham, Voddie. *Family Driven Faith: Doing What It Takes to Raise Sons and Daughters Who Walk with God.* Wheaton, IL: Crossway, 2007. Print

Baxter, Jeff. *Together: Adults and Teenagers Transforming the Church.* Grand Rapids, MI: Zondervan, 2010. Print.

Benson, Warren S., and Mark Senter. *The Complete Book of Youth Ministry.* Chicago: Moody, 1987. Print.

Bolsinger, Tod E. *It Takes a Church to Raise a Christian: How the Community of God Transforms Lives.* Grand Rapids, MI: Brazos, 2004. Print.

Bomar, Chuck. *College Ministry 101: a Guide to Working with 18-25 Year Olds.* Grand Rapids, MI: Zondervan, 2009. Print.

Bomar, Chuck. *College Ministry from Scratch: a Practical Guide to Start and Sustain a Successful College Ministry.* Grand Rapids, MI: Youth Specialties/Zondervan, 2010. Print.

Boshers, Bo and Judson Poling. *The Be-With Factor: Mentoring Students in Everyday Life.* Grand Rapids, MI: Zondervan, 2006. Print.

Brown, Scott T. *A Weed in the Church: How a Culture of Age Segregation Is Harming the Younger Generation, Fragmenting the Family, and Dividing the Church.* Wake Forest, NC: National Center for Family-Integrated Churches, 2010. Print.

Burns, Jim, and Mike DeVries. *Partnering with Parents in Youth Ministry.* Ventura, CA: Gospel Light, 2003. Print.

211

Calhoun, Mike, and Mel Walker. *Pushing the Limits: Unleashing the Potential of Student Ministry*. Nashville, TN: Thomas Nelson, 2006. Print.

Calhoun, Mike, and Mel Walker. *The Greenhouse Project: Cultivating Students of Influence*. Schroon Lake, NY: Word of Life Fellowship, 2009. Print.

Clark, Chap. *Hurt: Inside the World of Today's Teenagers*. Grand Rapids, MI: Baker Academic, 2004. Print.

Clinton, Hillary Rodham. *It Takes a Village: and Other Lessons Children Teach Us*. New York: Simon Schuster, 1996. Print.

Coleman, Robert E. *The Master Plan of Evangelism*. Grand Rapids, MI: Baker Publishing Group, 1972. Print.

Crawford, Dan D. *A Thirst for Souls: the Life of Evangelist Percy B. Crawford (1902-1960)*. Selinsgrove PA: Susquehanna UP, 2010. Print.

Dean, Kenda Creasy. *Almost Christian: What the Faith of Our Teenagers Is Telling the American Church*. Oxford: Oxford UP, 2010. Print.

DeVries, Mark. *Family-based Youth Ministry*. Downers Grove, IL: InterVarsity, 2004. Print.

Dunham, Craig R., and Doug Serven. *Twentysomeone: Finding Yourself in a Decade of Transition*. Colorado Springs, CO: WaterBrook, 2003. Print.

Dyck, Drew. *Generation Ex-Christian: Why Young Adults Are Leaving the Faith – and How to Bring Them Back*. Chicago: Moody, 2010. Print.

Elmore, Tim. *Generation IY: Our Last Chance to save Their Future*. Atlanta, GA.: Poet Gardener, 2010. Print.

Fox, J. Mark. *Family-Integrated Church: Healthy Families, Healthy Church*. Longwood, FL: Xulon, 2006. Print.

Freudenburg, Ben F., and Rick Lawrence. *The Family-Friendly Church*. Loveland, CO: Vital Ministry., 1998. Print.

Gillon, Steven M. *Boomer Nation: the Largest and Richest Generation Ever and How It Changed America*. New York: Free, 2004. Print.

Glenn, Mike, and Thom S. Rainer. *In Real Time: Authentic Young Adult Ministry as It Happens*. Nashville, TN: B H Group, 2009. Print.

Gloor, Peter A. *Swarm Creativity: Competitive Advantage through Collaborative Innovation Networks*. Oxford: Oxford UP, 2006. Print.

Guidry, Dustin. *Turning the Ship: Exploring the Age-Integrated Church*. Maitland, FL: Xulon Press, 2009. Print.

Ham, Ken, C. Britt. Beemer, and Todd A. Hillard. *Already Gone: Why Your Kids Will Quit Church and What You Can Do to Stop It*. Green Forest, AR: Master, 2009. Print.

Harry, Bollback. *The House That God Built: The Story of Jack Wyrtzen*. Schroon Lake, NY: Word of Life Fellowship, 1972. Print.

Haynes, Brian. *The Legacy Path: Discover Intentional Spiritual Parenting*. Nashville, TN: Randall House Publications, 2011. Print.

Hine, Thomas. *The Rise and Fall of the American Teenager*. New York: Avon , 1999. Print.

Holmen, Mark. *Church + Home: the Proven Formula for Building Lifelong Faith*. Ventura, CA: Regal, 2010. Print.

Howe, Neil, and William Strauss. *Millennials Go to College: Strategies for a New Generation on Campus: Recruiting and Admissions, Campus Life, and the Classroom*. Great Falls, VA: LifeCourse Associates, 2007. Print.

Howe, Neil, and William Strauss. *Millennials Rising: the next Great Generation /by Neil Howe and Bill Strauss ; Cartoons by R.J. Matson*. New York: Vintage, 2000. Print.

Howe, Neil, and William Strauss. *13th Gen: Abort, Retry, Ignore, Fail?* New York: Vintage . A Division of Random House, 1993. Print.

Hybels, Lynne, and Bill Hybels. *Rediscovering Church: the Story and Vision of Willow Creek Community Church*. Grand Rapids, MI: Zondervan, 1995. Print.

Joiner, Reggie. *Think Orange: Imagine the Impact When Church and Family Collide*. Colorado Springs, CO: David C. Cook, 2009. Print.

Kett, Joseph F. *Rites of Passage: Adolescence in America 1970 to the Present*. New York, NY: Basic Books (Harper Torch Books), 1977. Print.

Kimball, Dan. *They Like Jesus but Not the Church: Insights from Emerging Generations*. Grand Rapids, MI: Zondervan, 2007. Print.

Kinnaman, David. *You Lost Me: Why Young Christians are Leaving Church...and Rethinking Faith.* Grand Rapids, MI: Baker Books, 2011. Print.

Kirk, Brian, and Jacob Thorne. *Missional Youth Ministry: Moving from Gathering Teenagers to Scattering Disciples.* Grand Rapids, MI: Zondervan, 2011. Print.

Luce, Ron. *Revolution YM: the Complete Guide to High-impact Youth Ministry.* Colorado Springs, CO: NexGen, 2006. Print.

Lyons, Gabe. *The Next Christians: the Good News about the End of Christian America.* New York: Doubleday Religion, 2010. Print.

MacDonald, Gordon. *Who Stole My Church? What to Do When the Church You Love Tries to Enter the 21st Century.* Nashville, TN: Thomas Nelson, 2007. Print.

McIntosh, Gary. *One Church, Four Generations: Understanding and Reaching All Ages in Your Church.* Grand Rapids, MI: Baker, 2002. Print.

McKee, Jonathan R., and David R. Smith. *Ministry by Teenagers: Developing Leaders from within.* Grand Rapids, MI: Youth Specialties, 2011. Print.

Meredith, Char. *It' a Sin to Bore a Kid: The Story of Young Life.* Waco, TX: Word, 1978. Print.

Merritt, Carol Howard. *Tribal Church: Ministering to the Missing Generation.* Herndon, VA: Alban Institute, 2007. Print.

Mueller, Walt. *Understanding Today's Youth Culture.* Wheaton, IL: Tyndale House, 1999. Print.

Oestreicher, Mark. *Youth Ministry 3.0: a Manifesto of Where We've Been, Where We Are and Where We Need to Go.* Grand Rapids, MI: Zondervan, 2008. Print.

Powell, Brad. *Change Your Church for Good: The Art of Sacred Cow Tipping.* Nashville, TN: Thomas Nelson, 2007. Print.

Powell, Dr. Kara and Dr. Chap Clark. *Sticky Faith: Everyday Ideas to Build Lasting Faith in Your Kids.* Grand Rapids, MI: Zondervan, 2011. Print.

Powell, Dr. Kara, Brad Griffin, and Dr. Cheryl Crawford. *Sticky Faith (Youth Worker Edition): Practical Ideas to Mature Long-Term Faith in Teenagers.* Zondervan, Grand Rapids, MI, 2011. Print.

Rahn, Dave, and Terry Linhart. *Contagious Faith: Empowering Student Leadership in Youth Evangelism.* Loveland, CO: Group Pub., 2000. Print.

Rainer, Thom S., and Jess W. Rainer. *The Millennials: Connecting to America's Largest Generation*. Nashville, TN: BH Publishing Group, 2011. Print.

Rainer, Thom S., and Sam S. Rainer. *Essential Church? Reclaiming a Generation of Dropouts*. Nashville, TN: B H, 2008. Print.

Renfro, Paul, Brandon Shields, Jay Strother, and Timothy P. Jones. *Perspectives on Family Ministry: 3 Views*. Nashville, TN: B H Academic, 2009. Print.

Rice, Wayne. *Engaging Parents as Allies*. Cincinnati, OH: Standard Pub., 2009. Print.

Rice, Wayne. *Reinventing Youth Ministry (again): from Bells and Whistles to Flesh and Blood*. Downers Grove, IL: IVP, 2010. Print.

Root, Andrew, and Kenda Creasy Dean. *The Theological Turn in Youth Ministry*. Downers Grove, IL: IVP, 2011. Print.

Root, Andrew. *Revisiting Relational Youth Ministry: from a Strategy of Influence to a Theology of Incarnation*. Downers Grove, IL: IVP, 2007. Print.

Ryrie, Charles C. *A Survey of Bible Doctrine*. Chicago, IL: Moody, 1972. Print.

Sandler, Lauren. *Righteous: Dispatches from the Evangelical Youth Movement*. New York: Viking, 2006. Print.

Savage, Jon. *Teenage: the Creation of Youth Culture*. New York: Viking, 2007. Print.

Senter, Mark. *The Coming Revolution in Youth Ministry*. Wheaton, IL: Victor, 1992. Print.

Senter, Mark. *When God Shows Up: a History of Protestant Youth Ministry in America*. Grand Rapids, MI: Baker Academic, 2010. Print.

Smith, Christian, and Melinda Lundquist. Denton. *Soul Searching: the Religious and Spiritual Lives of American Teenagers*. Oxford: Oxford UP, 2005. Print.

Smith, Christian, and Patricia Snell. *Souls in Transition: the Religious and Spiritual Lives of Emerging Adults*. Oxford: Oxford UP, 2009. Print.

Smith, Christian, Kari Marie Christoffersen, Hilary Davidson, and Patricia Snell. Herzog. *Lost in Transition: the Dark Side of Emerging Adulthood*. New York: Oxford UP, 2011. Print.

Stetzer, Ed, Richie Stanley, and Jason Hayes. *Lost and Found: the Younger Unchurched and the Churches That Reach Them.* Nashville, TN: B H Pub. Group, 2009. Print.

Strauss, William, and Neil Howe. *The Fourth Turning: an American Prophecy.* New York: Broadway, 1997. Print.

Strauss, William, Neil Howe, and Peter George Markiewicz. *Millennials and the Pop Culture: Strategies for a New Generation of Consumers in Music, Movies, Television, the Internet, and Video Games.* Great Falls, VA: LifeCourse Associates, 2006. Print.

Wallace, Eric. *Uniting Church and Home: A Blueprint for Rebuilding Church Community.* Lorton, VA: Solutions for Integrating Church and Home, 1999.

Walker, Mel. *Impacting the Next Generation: a Strategy for Discipleship in Youth Ministry.* Schaumburg, IL: Regular Baptist, 2002. Print.

Walker, Mel. *Mentoring the Next Generation: a Strategy for Connecting the Generations.* Schaumburg, IL: Regular Baptist, 2003. Print.

Walker, Mel. *Reaching the Next Generation: Strategies for Evangelizing Today's Youth.* Schaumburg, IL: Regular Baptist, 2004. Print.

Warren, Richard. *The Purpose Driven Church: Growth without Compromising Your Message & Mission.* Grand Rapids, MI: Zondervan Pub., 1995. Print.

Winograd, Morley, and Michael D. Hais. *Millennial Momentum: How a New Generation Is Remaking America.* New Brunswick, NJ: Rutgers UP, 2011. Print.

Wright, Steve, and Chirs Graves. *ReThink: Decide for Yourself, Is Student Ministry Working?* Wake Forest, NC: InQuest, 2007. Print.

Endnotes

[1] Taken from http://dictionary.reference.com/browse/tradition.

[2] *Missional Youth Ministry: Moving from Gathering Teenagers to Scattering Disciples* by Brian Kirk and Jacob Thome (p. 140), published by Youth Specialties/Zondervan, Grand Rapids, MI, 2011.

[3] *Emerging Adulthood: The Winding Road from the Late Teens through the Twenties* by Jeffrey Jenson Arnett (p. 3-4), Oxford University Press, New York, NY, 2006.

[4] See *Generations: The History of America's Future, 1584 to 2069* by Neil Howe and William Strauss, published by Quill, 1992.

[5] http://www.youthministry.com/student-vs-youth-there-difference.

[6] *Intergenerational Ministry - Beyond the Rhetoric* by Brenda Snailum and Brad Griffin, 2011 Fuller Youth Institute: http://fulleryouthinstitute.org/2011/intergenerational-ministry-beyond-the-rhetoric/.

[7] *When did Sunday Schools Start?* by Timothy Larson: http://www.christianitytoday.com/ch/asktheexpert/whendidsundayschoolstart.html.

[8] *A Brief History of the Sunday School* by Jeri Tanner: http://ministry-to-children.com/history-of-sunday-school/

[9] http://en.wikipedia.org/wiki/Rite_of_passage.

[10] *The New Generation Gap* by Neil Howe and William Strauss in *The Atlantic Online:* http://www.theatlantic.com/past/issues/92dec/9212genx.htm.

[11] *Generations: The History of America's Future, 1584 to 2069* by William Strauss & Neil Howe (p. 25), published by William Morrow and Company, Inc., New York, 1991.

[12] A list of the Howe and Strauss books consulted for this book can be found in the bibliography. For more information see: http://www.lifecourse.com.

[13] *The Industrial Revolution* by Joseph A. Montagna: http://www.yale.edu/ynhti/curriculum/units/1981/2/81.02.06.x.html.

[14] http://www.educationbug.org/a/compulsory-education.html.

[15] http://www25.uua.org/uuhs/duub/articles/horacemann.html.

[16] *Rites of Passage: Adolescence in America 1790 to the Present* by Joseph F. Kett (p. 228), published by Basic Books, Inc. (Harper Torch Books), New York, 1977.

[17]

http://www.continuetolearn.uiowa.edu/laborctr/child_labor/about/us_history.html.

[18]

http://www.lawyershop.com/practice-areas/criminal-law/juvenile-law/history.

[19] *Is the Era of Age Segmentation Over?* A *Christianity Today* interview with Kara Powell:
http:///www.christianitytoday.com/le/2009/summer/istheearofagesegmentationover.html.

[20] http://www.infoplease.com/year/1944.html.

[21] *Teenage: The Creation of Youth Culture* by Jon Savage (p. 448), published by Viking, New York, 2007.

[22] *One Church Four Generations* by Gary McIntosh (p. 71), published by Baker Books, Grand Rapids, MI, 2002.

[23] *The Complete Book of Youth Ministry* edited by Warren Benson and Mark Senter III (p. 68), published by Moody Press, Chicago, 1987.

[24] *The Coming Revolution in Youth Ministry and Its Radical Impact on the Church* by Mark Senter III (p. 111), published by Victor Books (Scripture Press), Wheaton, IL, 1992.

[25] *Teenage: The Creation of Youth Culture* (p. 446).

[26] *The Coming Revolution in Youth Ministry* (p. 111).

[27] *Encyclopedia of Evangelicalism* (p. 774), on http://www.questia.com.

[28] http://www.wheaton.edu/bgc/archives/GUIDES/048.htm#41.

[29] *The Complete Book of Youth Ministry* (p. 70).

[30] For a general history of evangelical youth ministry see Mark Senter's books *The Coming Revolution in Youth Ministry* and *When God Shows Up*. More information is also available in Michael Loftis's unpublished doctoral dissertation, *A Historical Survey of Evangelical Youth Ministry in the United States,* Temple Baptist Theological Seminary, Chattanooga, TN, 1988.

[31] *The Coming Revolution in Youth Ministry* (p. 141).

32
http://www.liberty.edu/libertyjournal/index.cfm?PID=15758&section=8&artid=781&CFID=4958891&CFTOKEN=69365878.

33 *Ibid.*

34 See http://www.davidccook.com/About/about/index.cfm?N=7,167,2,1 for an example.

35 *When God Shows Up: A History of Protestant Youth Ministry in America* by Mark H. Senter III (p. 248), published by Baker Academic (Baker Books), Grand Rapids, MI, 2010.

36 *Soul Searching: The Religious and Spiritual Lives of American Teenagers* by Christian Smith (p. 32), published by Oxford University Press, 2005.

37 *The Coming Revolution in Youth Ministry* (p. 142).

38 *Growing Up Without Selling Out: The Professionalization of Youth Ministry* by Mark Cannister (p. 26), published in *YouthWorker Journal*, September/October 2005.

39 *Think Orange: Imagine the Impact When Church & Family Collide* by Reggie Joiner (p. 49-50), published by David C. Cook, Colorado Springs, CO, 2009.

40 *A Survey of Bible Doctrine* by Charles C. Ryrie (p. 140), published by Moody Publishers, Chicago, IL, 1972.

41 *The Church in God's Program* by Robert L. Saucy (in Preface), published by Moody Publishers, Chicago, IL, 1972.

42 *Rediscovering Church: The Story and Vision of Willow Creek Community Church* by Lynne and Bill Hybels (p. 169), published by Zondervan Publishing House, Grand Rapids, MI, 1995.

43 *It Takes a Church to Raise a Christian: How the Community of God Transforms Lives* by Tod E. Bolsinger (p. 22), published by Brazos Press (a division of Baker Book House), Grand Rapids, MI, 2004.

44 *A Survey of Bible Doctrine* by Charles C. Ryrie (p. 154).

45 *They Like Jesus But Not The Church: Insights from Emerging Generations* by Dan Kimball, published by Zondervan, Grand Rapdis, MI, 2007.

46 *It Takes a Church to Raise a Christian: How the Community of God Transforms Lives* by Tod E. Bolsinger (p. 22).

[47] *Already Gone: Why Your Kids Will Quit Church & What You Can Do to Stop It"* by Ken Ham (p. 119), published by Master Books, Green Forest, AR, 2009.

[48] *Already Gone: Why Your Kids Will Quit Church & What You Can Do to Stop It"* by Ken Ham (p. 118).

[49] *They Like Jesus But Not The Church: Insights from Emerging Generations* by Dan Kimball (p. 16), published by Zondervan, Grand Rapids, MI, 2007.

[50] *Swarm Creativity: Competitive Advantage through Collaborative Innovation Networks* by Peter A. Gloor, published by Oxford University Press, New York, NY, 2006.

[51] *The 7 Habits of Highly Effective People* by Stephen R. Covey, published by Free Press/Simon and Shuster, New York, NY, 1998, 2004.

[52] *Swarm Creativity: Competitive Advantage through Collaborative Innovation Networks* by Peter A. Gloor (p. 22).

[53] *Think Orange: Imagine the Impact When Church & Family Collide* by Reggie Joiner (p. 25).

[54] http://www.christianitytoday.com/ct/2005/julyweb-only/22.0.html.

[55] Ibid.

[56] *Together: Adults and Teenagers Transforming the Church* by Jeff Baxter (p. 25), published by Youth Specialties/Zondervan, Grand Rapids, MI, 2010.

[57] *Already Gone: Why Your Kids Will Quit Church & What You Can Do to Stop It* by Ken Ham (p. 31).

[58] See *Simple Church: Returning to God's Process for Making Disciples* by Thom S. Rainer and Eric Geiger, published by B&H Books, 2011.

[59] http://www.ncfic.org/.

[60] http://www.barna.org/barna-update/article/5-barna-update/126-small-churches-struggle-to-grow-because-of-the-people-they-attract?q=church+attendance+size.

[61] http://www.outreachmagazine.com/features/3769-Largest-and-Fastest-Growing-Churches-America.html.

[62] Ibid.

[63] *A Weed in the Church: How a Culture of Age Segregation is Destroying the Younger Generation, Fragmenting the Family, and Diving the Church* by Scott T. Brown (p. 113), published by the National Center for Family-Integrated Churches, Wake Forest, NC, 2011.

[64] *Together: Adults and Teenagers Transforming the Church* by Jeff Baxter (p. 150-151).

[65] http://www.youngchurch.org/.

[66] http://marshill.org/history/.

[67] http://fulleryouthinstitute.org/2010/08/moving-away-from-the-kid-table/.

[68] *Hurt: Inside the World of Today's Teenagers* by Chap Clark (p. 190), published by Baker Academic/Baker Publishing Group, Grand Rapids, MI, 2004.

[69] Ibid.

[70] http://www.christianitytoday.com/le/communitylife/discipleship/istheeraofage segmentationover.html.

[71] *Family-Driven Faith: Doing What It Takes to Raise Sons and Daughters Who Walk with God* by Voddie Baucham Jr., published by Crossway Books, Wheaton, IL, 2007.

[72] *A Weed in the Church: How a Culture of Age Segregation is Destroying the Younger Generation, Fragmenting the Family, and Dividing the Church* by Scott T. Brown.

[73] *Sticky Faith: Everyday Ideas to Build Lasting Faith in Your Kids* by Kara Powell and Chap Clark (p. 96), published by Zondervan, Grand Rapids, MI, 2011.

[74] *Transforming Children into Spiritual Champions* by George Barna (cover and p. 11), Ventura, CA: Regal Books, 2003.

[75] http://www.barna.org/barna-update/article/5-barna-update/196-evangelism-is-most-effective-among-kids?q=age+salvation.

[76] *Transforming Children into Spiritual Champions* by George Barna (p. 45).

[77] *Think Orange: Imagine the Impact When Church and Family Collide* by Reggie Joiner, published by David C. Cook, Colorado Springs, CO, 2009.

[78] http://whatisorange.org/about-orange-strategy/.

[79] http://en.wikipedia.org/wiki/Curriculum.

[80] *Pushing the Limits: Unleashing the Potential of Student Ministry* by Mike Calhoun and Mel Walker, published by Nelson Books/Thomas Nelson Publishing, Nashville, TN, 2006.

[81] See http://www.time.com/time/magazine/article/0,9171,1940697,00.html for an interesting cultural take on the topic of "helicopter parents."

[82] See http://www.markgr.com/get-ready-for-stealth-fighter-parents/.

[83] *Millennials Go to College: Strategies for a New Generation on Campus* by Neil Howe and William Strauss, published by American Association of Collegiate Registrars, 2003.

[84] For example see http://www.brotherhoodmutual.com/index.cfm/resources/background-screening.

[85] http://www.barna.org/teens-next-gen-articles/147-most-twentysomethings-put-christianity-on-the-shelf-following-spiritually-active-teen-years.

[86] For example see *A Weed in the Church* by Scott Brown, and Voddie Baucham's podcast entitled "*Youth Ministry*" available on iTunes.

[87] *Contagious Faith: Empowering Student Leadership in Youth Evangelism* by Dave Rahn and Terry Linhart (p. 19), published by Group Publishing, Loveland, CO, 2000.

[88] http://www.christianitytoday.com/ct/2005/julyweb-only/22.0.html.

[89] *Contagious Faith: Empowering Student Leadership in Youth Evangelism* by Dave Rahn and Terry Linhart (p. 19).

[90] For more information on the history of evangelical youth ministry see Mark Senter's books *The Coming Revolution in Youth Ministry* and *When God Shows Up.* I also recommend *A Thirst for Souls: The Life of Evangelist Percy B. Crawford* by Dan Crawford (Susquehanna University Press, 2010), and *The House That God Built: The Story of Jack Wyrtzen* by Harry Bollback (published by Word of Life Fellowship, 1998) for encouraging historical narratives of some of the early leaders of evangelical youth ministry.

[91] *Contagious Faith: Empowering Student Leadership in Youth Evangelism* by Dave Rahn and Terry Linhart (p. 19).

92 The *National Center for Family-Integrated Churches* has released a scathing, yet professionally-done video presenting a series of so-called weaknesses within traditional youth ministry – see http://www.dividedthemovie.com/ or https://www.ncfic.org/divided. Although I disagree with the premise and many of the arguments in this presentation, it is well done and will help viewers understand the anti youth ministry positions of the *family-integrated church* movement.

93 *A Weed in the Church: How a Culture of Age Segregation is Destroying the Younger Generation, Fragmenting the Family, and Dividing the Church* by Scott T. Brown (p. 33).

94 Ibid (p. 34).

95 Ibid (see the chapter title on p. 33).

96 Personal e-mail from a friend in youth ministry (dated August 16, 2011).

97 Out of my respect for this person's ministry I am not going to quote him by name in this book.

98 See http://www.wol.org/.

99 See http://positiveaction.org/.

100 See http://www.sonlifeclassic.com/.

101 The Association of Youth Ministry Educators is a professional association organized for those teaching youth ministry on the college or seminary level. See http://www.aymeducators.org/.

102 *Pushing the Limits: Unleashing the Potential of Student Ministry* by Mike Calhoun and Mel Walker (p. 83), published by Thomas Nelson Publishing, Nashville, TN, 2006.

103 http://awana.org/on/demandware.store/Sites-Awana-Site/default/Default-Start.

104 http://quiettimediary.com/.

105 *reThink: Decide for Yourself, is Student Ministry Working?* by Steve Wright with Chris Graves (p. 144), published by InQuest Publishing, Wake Forest, NC, 2008.

106 See http://www.youthworker.com/youth-ministry-resources-ideas/youth-ministry/11623973/.

107 *Partnering with Parents in Youth Ministry* by Jim Burns and Mike DeVries, published by Gospel Light, Ventura, CA, 2003.

[108] *Church + Home: The Proven Formula for Building Lifelong Faith* by Mark Holmen, published by Regal/Gospel Light, Ventura, CA, 2010.

[109] See *A Thirst for Souls: The Life of Evangelist Percy B. Crawford* by Dan Crawford, published by Susquehanna University Press, 2010, and *When God Shows Up: A History of Protestant Youth Ministry in America* by Mark H. Senter III, published by Baker Academic/Baker Books, Grand Rapids, MI, 2010.

[110] See *It's a Sin to Bore a Kid* by Char Meredith, published by Word Books, Waco, Texas, 1978.

[111] *When God Shows Up: A History of Protestant Youth Ministry in America* by Mark H. Senter III (p. 263).

[112] A secular, scathing critique of the large youth event movement can be found in: *Righteous: Dispatches from the Evangelical Youth Movement* by Lauren Sandler, published by Viking/Penguin Group, New York, NY, 2006.

[113] See *A Thirst for Souls: The Life of Evangelist Percy B. Crawford* by Dan Crawford, published by Susquehanna University Press, 2010.

[114] See http://www.ccca.org/public/education/102timeline.asp.

[115] *A Thirst for Souls: The Life of Evangelist Percy B. Crawford* by Dan Crawford (p. 233-234).

[116] *Outbreak: Creating a Contagious Youth Ministry Through Viral Evangelism* by Greg Stier, published by Moody Publishers, 2006.

[117] I wrote a practical handbook for youth workers on how to implement an evangelistic strategy in their youth groups entitled, *Reaching the Next Generation: Strategies for Evangelizing Today's Youth* by Mel Walker, published by Regular Baptist Press, Schaumburg, IL, 2004.

[118] http://www.christianitytoday.com/ct/2005/julyweb-only/22.0.html.

[119] For examples of some of the products available to help youth workers with short-term missions trips see *Mission Trip Prep Kit Leader's Guide* by Kevin Johnson, published by Zondervan/Youth Specialties, 2003, and *The Essential Guide to the Short Term Mission Trips* by David C. Forward, published by Moody Publishers, 1998.

[120]
http://www.christianendeavor.com/index.php?option=com_content&view=article&id=132&Itemid=150.

[121] For example see *Spiritual Formation as if the Church Mattered: Growing in Christ through Community* by James C. Wilhoit, published by Baker Academic/Baker Publishing Group, Grand Rapids, MI, 2008.

122 Reprinted at:
http://inthelandofoz.blogspot.com/2006/06/hurried-discipleship-mike-yaconell i-i.html.

123 For specific information on how to implement discipleship in youth ministry see *Impacting the Next Generation: A Strategy for Discipleship in Youth Ministry* by Mel Walker, published by Regular Baptist Press, Schaumburg, IL, 2002.

124 Here are some examples of books on the subject of relational youth ministry: *Revisiting Relational Youth Ministry: From a Strategy of Influence to a Theology of Incarnation* by Andrew Root, published by IVP Books, 2007; *The Youth Builder: Today's Resource for Relationship Youth Ministry* by Jim Burns and Mike DeVries, published by Gospel Light Publications, 2002.

125 For specific information on how to implement a mentoring ministry in youth ministry, see *Mentoring the Next Generation: A Strategy for Connecting the Generations* by Mel Walker, published by Regular Baptist Press, Schaumburg, IL, 2003.

126 *Essential Church? Reclaiming a Generation of Dropouts* by Thom S. Rainer and Sam S. Rainer III (p. 2), published by B&H Publishing Group, Nashville, TN, 2008.

127 Ibid (p. 14).

128 *You Lost Me: Why Young Christians Are Leaving the Church...And Rethinking Faith* by David Kinnaman (p. 22), published by Baker Books, Grand Rapids, MI, 2011.

129 http://www.bls.gov/news.release/pdf/hsgec.pdf.

130 *Millennials Go To College: Strategies for a New Generation on Campus* by Neil Howe and William Strauss (p. 35), published by Lifecourse Associates, 2007.

131 *Rediscovering Church* by Bill and Lynne Hybels, published by Zondervan, Grand Rapids, MI, 1997.

132 http://www.barna.org/teens-next-gen-articles/492-what-teens-aspire-to-do-in-life-how-churches-can-help?q=teens+aspire.

133 Quotation from Krish Kandiah in *Lost Me: Why Young Christians Are Leaving the Church...And Rethinking Faith* by David Kinnaman (p. 216).

134 http://stickyfaith.org/.

135 http://nces.ed.gov/fastfacts/display.asp?id=98.

136
http://pewresearch.org/pubs/1391/college-enrollment-all-time-high-community-college-surge.

137 http://www.insidehighered.com/news/2008/08/22/growth.

138 http://nces.ed.gov/fastfacts/display.asp?id=74.

139 http://stickyfaith.org/blog/college-ministry-for-high-school-pastors.

140 *College Ministry 101: A Guide to Working with 18-25 Year Olds* by Chuck Bomar (p. 24), published by Youth Specialties/Zondervan, Grand Rapids, MI, 2009.

141 http://www.nytimes.com/2010/08/22/magazine/22Adulthood-t.html.

142 Ibid http://www.nytimes.com/2010/08/22/magazine/22Adulthood-t.html.

143 See *Emerging Adulthood: The Winding Road from the Late Teens through the Twenties* by Jeffrey Jensen Arnett, published by Oxford University Press, New York, NY, 2004.

144 Referring to Mars Hill church near Grand Rapids, MI. See http://stickyfaith.org.blog/college-ministry-for-high-school-pastors.

145 *College Ministry 101: A Guide to Working with 18-25 Year Olds* by Chuck Bomar (p. 26).

146 Ibid (p. 24).

147 www.babyzone.com/mom_dad/quiz/helicopter-parent (Note: this web site contains an interesting quiz, *Are You a Helicopter Parent?*).

148 *The Trophy Kids Grow Up: How the Millennial Generation is Shaking Up the Workplace* by Ron Alsop (p. 56), Jossey-Bass, San Francisco, CA, 2008.

149 Ibid (p. 55).

150 *College Ministry 101: A Guide to Working with 18-25 Year Olds* by Chuck Bomar (p. 24).

151 http://www.infoplease.com/ipa/A0005061.html.

152 http://www.nytimes.com/2010/08/22/magazine/22Adulthood-t.html.

153
http://www.washingtonpost.com/wp-srv/special/politics/dont-ask-dont-tell-timeline.

154 http://www.reuters.com/article/2011/06/25/us-gaymarriage-usa-idUSTRE75O 0G420110625.

155 http://www.nytimes.com/2010/07/07/business/economy/07generation.html.

156 http://www.nytimes.com/2010/08/22/magazine/22Adulthood-t.html?pagewant ed=print.

157 A recent University of Michigan study also presents the viewpoint that this trend could be positive for emerging adults. See http://www.minnpost.com/healthblog/2011/03/17/26691/young_adults_help_f rom_parents_doesnt_mean_theyre_slackers_u_of_m_study_finds.

158 *Lost Me: Why Young Christians Are Leaving the Church...And Rethinking Faith* by David Kinnaman (p. 19).

159 The *"Passion"* conferences are one example of this movement that featured an emphasis upon young adults. See the story at: http://mnnonline.org/article/15178 and http://www.268generation.com/3.0/#!about/story.

"/>160 *Change Your Church for Good: The Art of Sacred Cow Tipping* by Brad Powell (p.33), published by Thomas Nelson: Nashville, TN, 2007.

160 *Who Stole My Church? What to Do When the Church You Love Tries to Enter the 21st Century* by Gordon MacDonald, published by Thomas Nelson: Nashville, TN, 2007.

161 *The Trophy Kids Grow Up: How the Millennial Generation is Shaking Up the Workplace* by Ron Alsop (p. 220), published by Jossey-Bass: San Francisco, CA, 2008.

162 *The Millennials: Connecting to America's Largest Generation* by Thom Rainer and Jess Rainer (p. 114), published by BH Publishing Group: Nashville, TN, 2011.

163 Ibid (p. 115.)

164 *Hurt: Inside the World of Today's Teenagers* by Chap Clark (p. 190), published by Baker Academic/Baker Publishing Group, Grand Rapids, MI, 2004.

165 See *Rites of Passage: Adolescence in America 1790 to the Present* by Joseph F. Kett, published by Basic Books, Inc. (Harper Torch Books), New York, 1977.

[166] For further reading on the importance of a curriculum in church ministry, see my chapter "Teaching on Purpose with a Purpose" in *Pushing the Limits: Unleashing the Potential of Student Ministry* edited by Mike Calhoun and Mel Walker, published by Thomas Nelson, 2006.

[167] See *Introducing Christian Education: Foundations for the Twenty-First Century* edited by Michael J. Anthony, published by Baker Academic: Grand Rapids, MI, 2001.

[168] http://family.jrank.org/pages/1222/Nuclear-Families.html.

[169] See http://www.childstats.gov/americaschildren/famsoc1.asp.

[170] *Millennials Go To College* by Neil Howe and William Strauss (p. 35), published by Lifecourse Associates, 2007.

[171] For example see http://christwayministries.us/deacon-caring-ministry-seminar.

[172] *Lost and Found: The Younger Unchurched and the Churches That Reach Them* by Ed Stetzer, Richie Stanley, and Jason Hayes (p. 129), published by BH Publishing Group LifeWay Research, Nashville, TN, 2009.

[173] http://seniorjournal.com/NEWS/SeniorStats/2011/20110527-NationsPopulationAging.htm.

[174] *The Millennials: Connecting to America's Largest Generation* by Thom Rainer and Jess W. Rainer (p. 2), published by BH Publishing Group, Nashville, TN, 2011.

[175] For a helpful article with the same basic analogy see http://fulleryouthinstitute.org/2010/08/moving-away-from-the-kid-table/.

[176] Church leaders and youth workers should read: *Better Safe Than Sued: Keeping Your Students and Ministry Safe* by Jack Crabtreee, published by Zondervan/Youth Specialties, Grand Rapids, MI, 2008.

[177] For an example of what is available for churches on this subject see http://www.brotherhoodmutual.com/index.cfm/resources/ministry-safety/children-youth/.

[178] Again, for specific information on how to implement a mentoring ministry in youth ministry see *Mentoring the Next Generation: A Strategy for Connecting the Generations* by Mel Walker, published by Regular Baptist Press, Schaumburg, IL, 2003.

[179] Much of this chapter is adapted from the authors' chapter in *The Greenhouse Project: Cultivating Students of Influence* by Mike Calhoun and Mel Walker, published by Word of Life Fellowship, Schroon Lake, NY, 2009 (Used by permission).

[180] *Essential Church? Reclaiming a Generation of Dropouts* by Thom Rainer and Sam Rainer III (p. 2, 15), published by BH Publishing, Nashville, TN, 2008.

[181] *Who Stole My Church? What to do When the Church You Love Tries to Enter the 21st Century* by Gordon MacDonald (p. *viii*), published by Thomas Nelson, Nashville, TN, (reprint edition) 2010.

[182] http://www.christianitytoday.com/le/2002/spring/4.43.html?start=2.

[183] *ReThink: Decide for Yourself, Is Student Ministry Working* by Steve Wright (p. 31), published by InQuest Ministries. Wake Forest, NC, 2007.

[184] See *Soul Searching: the Religious and Spiritual Lives of American Teenagers* by Christian Smith and Melinda L. Denton, published by Oxford University Press, New York, NY, 2009.

[185] *One Church, Four Generations* by Gary McIntosh (p. 221), published by Baker Books, Grand Rapids, MI, 2002.

[186] See the author's book *Mentoring the Next Generation: A Strategy for Connecting the Generations* published by Regular Baptist Press, Schaumburg, IL, 2003.

[187] *Perspective on Family Ministry: 3 Views* by Paul Renfro, Brandon Shields, and Jay Strother, edited by Timothy Paul Jones, published by BH Publishing Group, Nashville, TN, 2009.

[188] Ibid (p. 52).

[189] See http://www.gracefamilybaptist.net/voddie-baucham-ministries/.

[190] *Family Driven Faith* by Voddie Baucham (p. 191-195).

[191] http://dividedthemovie.com/.

[192] http://www.youthministry.com/articles/leadership/defense-youth-ministry.

[193] See *Purpose Driven Church: Growth Without Compromising Your Message Mission* by Rick Warren, published by Zondervan, Grand Rapids, MI, 2002.

[194] *Word Studies in the New Testament, Volume III, The Epistles of Paul* by Marvin R. Vincent (p. 404), published by Eerdmans Publishing Co., Grand Rapids, MI, reprinted 1975.

195
http://www.barna.org/barna-update/article/5-barna-update/120-parents-accept-responsibility-for-their-childs-spiritual-development-but-struggle-with-effectiveness?q=parents+accept+responsibility.

[196] For an example, see the main outline in this article: http://fulleryouthinstitute.org/2008/11/theological-principles-behind-intergenerational-youth-ministry/.

[197] http://abcnews.go.com/topics/lifestyle/divorce-rates.htm.

[198] For example see http://www.philly.com/philly/opinion/20120518_Same-sex_marriage__Who_says_it_rsquo_s_a_right_.html.

[199] http://www.myspace.com/intgd/splash.html.

[200] See http://www.ncfic.org/about_the_board.

[201] *A Weed in the Church: How a Culture of Age Segregation is Destroying the Younger Generation, Fragmenting the Family, and Dividing the Church* by Scott T. Brown (p.141), published by the National Center for Family-Integrated Churches, Wake Forest, NC, 2011.

[202] *The Master Plan of Evangelism*, by Robert E. Coleman. Published by Fleming H. Revell (a division of Baker Publishing Group), Grand Rapids, MI, 1972.

[203] http://www.taketheleap.com/define.html.

[204] http://www.churchtimeline.com/ChurchTimeline.pdf.

[205] *Turning the Ship: Exploring the Age-Integrated Church* by Dustin Guidry (p. XIV), published by Xulon Press, Maitland, FL, 2009.

[206] *You Lost Me. Why Young Christians Are Leaving Church…And Rethinking Faith*, by David Kinnaman (p. 12-13), published by Baker Books, Grand Rapids, MI, 2011.

[207] http://www.brainyquote.com/quotes/quotes/a/alberteins133991.html.

[208] *The MacArthur New Testament Commentary: Acts 1-12* by John MacArthur, Jr. (p. 182), published by Moody Press, Chicago, IL, 1994.

[209] See *A Weed in the Church: How a Culture of Age Segregation is Harming the Younger Generation, Fragmenting the Family, and Dividing the Church* by Scott T. Brown.

[210] I will keep the identity of this church confidential out of respect for the long-term reputation of their ministry.

211 *The MacArthur New Testament Commentary: Ephesians,* by John MacArthur, Jr. (p. 152), published by Moody Press, Chicago, IL, 1986.

212 *Mentoring the Next Generation: A Strategy for Connecting the Generations* by Mel Walker, published by Regular Baptist Press, Schaumburg, IL, 2003.

213 See http://www.youtube.com/watch?v=fW8amMCVAJQ.

214 http://sivers.org/ff.

215 See http://en.wikipedia.org/wiki/Throw_out_the_baby_with_the_bath_water.

216 http://www.youthministry.com/articles/small-groups/why-go-small-groups.

217 For example see Bo Boshers's article at: http://www.youthworkers.net/index.cfm?fuseaction=netmag.viewarticleArticleID=112, and his book on the same theme: *The Be-With Factor: Mentoring Students in Everyday Life* by Bo Boshers and Judson Poling, published by Zondervan, Grand Rapids, MI, 2006.

218 *One Church – Four Generations: Understanding and Reaching All Ages in Your Church* by Gary L. McIntosh (p. 221-222), published by Baker Books, Grand Rapids, MI, 2002.

219 http://www.talentzoo.com/beneath-the-brand/blog_news.php?articleID=11654.

220 *Hurt: Inside the World of Today's Teenagers* by Chap Clark (p. 190), published by Baker Academic/Baker Publishing Group, Grand Rapids, MI, 2004.

221 Especially see Chapter 5: "A Sticky Web of Relationships" in *Sticky Faith: Everyday Ideas to Build Lasting Faith in Your Kids* by Kara Powell and Chap Clark (p. 93-121), published by Zondervan, Grand Rapids, MI, 2011

Made in the USA
Middletown, DE
05 March 2016